FORWARD

FORWARD EVER

The Life of
Kwame Nkrumah

School Edition

by the Editors of
Panaf Books

Panaf Books

Forward Ever

© Panaf Books

First published in 1977
Reprinted 2006

ISBN: 0 901787 42 6

Panaf Books
75 Weston Street
London SE1 3RS

Contents

'Today we are free.'
Kwame Nkrumah declares the independence of Ghana, 6 March 1957

1: Growing up

On 6 March 1957 there was great excitement in Ghana. For it was then that the people of Ghana became free to govern themselves. The British, who had for a long time ruled over the country, saw the flag of Britain lowered, and the new red, gold and green flag of Ghana raised in its place.

'Now we are free. Today we are free,' the people shouted. They danced and sang in the streets. Everyone was happy. But the happiest man of all was Kwame Nkrumah. His name was on everybody's lips, because all knew that he had worked harder than anyone else to free their country from colonial rule.

'At long last the battle has ended', Nkrumah told the thousands who had gathered in Accra to celebrate independence, 'and thus Ghana, our beloved country is free for ever.'

The people cheered and clapped. But Nkrumah went on to tell them of the hard work and struggles which lay ahead. He said that the winning of freedom to govern was only a beginning: 'For the independence of Ghana is meaningless unless it is linked up with the total liberation of the African continent.' The people of Ghana, he said, through work and sacrifice must make their country strong and self-reliant. They would then be able to help other peoples in Africa still suffering under foreign rule. There must be no relaxing until the whole continent of Africa was free and united.

Among the crowds listening to Kwame Nkrumah on that special day was his mother, Nyaniba. She was then an old lady, and nearly blind, but the sound of her son's voice, and the cheers of the people made her very happy. She remembered how she used to worry about her son when he was a child. He ate very little food, and she used to put a baked plantain under his pillow each night in case he woke up and felt hungry. She never thought that he would grow up to become a great leader.

He was her only child, and was born in the village of Nkroful in western Ghana on 18 September 1909. Until he was three years old, he lived with his mother in Nkroful. Then they went to join his father who was a goldsmith in Half Assini. He was a kind man, but was always very busy making gold and silver ornaments. So the young Nkrumah continued to keep close to his mother.

Although there were plenty of children to play with in Half Assini, Nkrumah sometimes complained to Nyaniba that she had given him no brothers and sisters. Once when he complained, she pointed to the forest and said: 'You see the big trees? They stand alone.'

He spent many happy hours playing with other children on the seashore, by the lagoon and in the forest. But best of all he liked to wander off on his own to observe the birds, the insects and the many small animals which lived in the forest. Often he would go all day without food, and would not return home until it was dark. Sometimes he carried a squirrel, a bird, a landcrab or some other small creature which he wanted to keep as a pet.

Soon the time came for him to go to school. On the first day he was so disappointed that he ran home, determined never to return. But Nyaniba took him back again the next morning, and as the days passed he began to enjoy his lessons.

In his school there was only one room, and one teacher for four classes. So the master had to teach each class in turn. Often, while he was teaching one class, the other children would chatter and waste time. This made him very angry, and he would beat them with a stick. Nkrumah thought he used the stick too much. Therefore, when an inspector was due to visit the school, he urged all the children to stay away for the whole day. In this way they thought they would get their revenge on the master. The following day, when the inspector arrived, he found no children in the school. Instead of sitting at their desks they were playing in the forest. Next day, the teacher was waiting for them with his stick, and he beat every one of them.

As he grew older, Nkrumah became so good at his lessons that he helped to teach the younger children. He was not very tall and had to stand on a box to write on the blackboard.

One day, the principal of a training college for teachers visited the school. He saw Nkrumah, who was then seventeen, teaching the younger children, and asked him if he would like to train to become a real teacher. The Teachers' Training College was in Accra, the capital city of Ghana, and a long way from Half Assini. But Nkrumah gladly agreed to go.

The following year, in 1927, he said goodbye to his parents and set out for Accra. It was a long and tiring journey because in those days there were few roads, and he had to walk most of the way.

Nkrumah had never been to Accra, and at first he felt very strange. He was amazed to see the crowded streets, the big buildings and the many shops. Accra seemed so noisy. But he soon got used to it, and within a short time settled down to his studies at the training college.

The assistant vice-principal of the college was Dr Kwegyir Aggrey, one of the finest teachers in Africa. His classes were always full, and whenever he spoke at public meetings thousands gathered to hear him. They listened to every word as he told them about the great achievements of the African people long before the arrival of Europeans in Africa. While he never spoke against foreigners simply because they belonged to another race, Dr Aggrey urged his students to work hard so that they could help Africans to be free once again.

At that time, most of the countries of Africa were ruled by foreigners and were therefore called 'colonies'. When Ghana was a colony of Britain it was known as the Gold Coast. It only came to be called 'Ghana' in 1957 at independence. 'Ghana' was the name of a great empire which existed in West Africa many hundreds of years ago.

Nkrumah was so inspired by the teaching of Dr Aggrey that he planned to devote his life to helping to achieve the wonderful future for his country and for the whole of Africa which Dr Aggrey so vividly described. He decided he must first complete his course at the training college. Then he must teach for a time in order to earn enough to pay for further education in a university overseas, because there was then no university in Ghana. Dr Aggrey had studied at an American university, and Nkrumah thought he would also like to study there.

A Nigerian called Nnamdi Azikwe also advised Nkrumah to go to America. Azikwe was at that time writing for a newspaper, *The African Morning Post*. Zik, as his friends called him, had himself studied at an American university. He returned to Africa from the USA in 1934, and worked to free Nigeria from British colonial rule. When the Nigerian people became free to govern themselves in 1960, Zik was declared governor-general.

Meantime, Nkrumah studied hard at the training college in Accra. The teachers considered him one of their best students. He was also good at sport. He could run very fast, and soon became a member of the athletics team. But more than anything else, Nkrumah liked to take part in the debates of the Aggrey Students' Society. He enjoyed speaking, and found that others enjoyed listening to him.

In 1928 the Accra Training College became part of the Prince of Wales College, a large secondary school in Achimota, a few miles from Accra. At Achimota, the student teachers lived side by side with the school students, and they learned a lot from each other.

In 1930, when he completed his training, Nkrumah became a teacher at the Roman Catholic Junior School in Elmina. A year later, he was promoted to be head teacher of the Junior School at Axim, where he spent the next two years. It was at this time that he decided to try to obtain a place at Lincoln University in the United States of America. On the entry form he was asked to give details of his education, and the reason for wanting to enter Lincoln University. He wrote:

'In all things I have held myself to but one ambition, and that is, to make necessary arrangements to continue my education in a university of the United States of America, that I may be better prepared, and still be of better use to my fellow men.'

After a short account of his education and teaching experience, he ended:

'Such is the brief history of my life, and I am forced to conclude with the same words: "So much to do, so little done." '

When news arrived that he had been accepted at Lincoln University, he was teaching at Amissano near Elmina. He was very excited. But he had not been able to save enough money to pay for the fare to the USA. He therefore decided to seek the help of an uncle who lived in Lagos, the capital city of Nigeria. Not having money for the ticket, Nkrumah hid in the boiler room of a ship which was about to sail for Lagos. It was a very uncomfortable voyage. The boiler room was airless and hot, and Nkrumah had very little to eat or drink. However, within a few days the ship docked in Lagos, and he was able to creep out of the boiler room and to run ashore without anyone seeing him.

His uncle, who was very surprised to see him, gave him some money. This together with his own savings was enough to pay for a ticket to Britain, and from Britain to the USA. Nkrumah had to go to Britain on his way to the USA in order to obtain the necessary travel documents.

The time came for Nkrumah to say goodbye to his mother. Although Nyaniba was very sad to think that it would be many years before she would see her son again, she did not try to persuade him not to go. They sat up all night talking. Then when day came Nkrumah packed his things into a canoe to begin the first part of his journey to the port of Takoradi. With tears in her eyes Nyaniba wished him well:

'May God and your ancestors guide you,' she said.

2 : Student days in America and Britain

When Nkrumah arrived in America at the end of October 1935, he had very little money. The cost of the long sea journey had left him with not enough to pay his college fees. To make matters worse, the term had already begun at Lincoln University.

Nkrumah told the Dean of the college that he would work very hard to catch up with the other students, and to earn enough to pay the college fees. The Dean therefore said that he could stay since he had travelled such a long way, and was so determined to do well. But first he would have to pass the college examinations.

At once Nkrumah set to work. He worked so hard that he gained high marks in the examinations, and won a scholarship. This helped to pay his college fees. But it was not enough for all his expenses. So he had to find ways to earn more money.

During term-time he earned a little by working in the college library, and by helping to serve meals in the dining hall. But during the holidays he had to do many other kinds of work.

He tried selling fish in the streets of New York. Early every morning he went to the fish market. But he could not sell enough to make any money. Then he found work in a soap factory. He thought that this would be a nice clean job. But he had forgotten that soap is made from animal fat, and this has a very nasty smell. Each day, lorries brought loads of animal fat into the yard of the soap factory. Nkrumah was given a large fork and was told to load the horrible fat into a wheelbarrow. He then had to wheel it into the factory. The smell made him feel so sick that after a few weeks a doctor advised him to leave.

He then decided to go to sea. For a time he worked as a dish-washer and a waiter on various ships. He did not mind the hard work because he liked seeing new places.

One year, he took a job in a shipyard. It was winter-time and he had to work during the night outside in the icy cold. He did not have enough thick clothes to keep him warm. Night after night when it rained or snowed, he shivered in the bitter cold. Soon he became ill. He was rushed to hospital where he nearly died.

There were times when he had hardly any money and could not find work. So he could not afford even to rent a room. He tried to sleep on a bench at a railway station or in a park. One night, when it was very cold, he decided to spend the night on one of the under-ground trains going backwards and forwards between Harlem and Brooklyn, two districts of New York. A single ticket cost little. But Nkrumah was not able to sleep much because each time the train reached the end of the line he had to slip into another coach without being seen by the guard. If the guard had seen him he would have made him buy another ticket.

Although Nkrumah spent much of his time in America working at various jobs, he never neglected his studies. At Lincoln and at the University of Philadelphia he studied theology, sociology, philosophy, economics and education. He obtained a Bachelor of Theology degree, a Master of Science degree in education, and a Master of Arts degree in philosophy. He made a particular study of the history of the African people. He wanted to find out all about how colonies were formed, and why the African people still suffered under foreign rule. He thought that if he knew the reasons for colonialism, its strength and its weaknesses, then he would be in a better position to work on the problem of how to end it.

As he studied, he began to write a book. This was first printed in 1945 and called *Towards Colonial Freedom*. In this book, Nkrumah wrote about the causes and the results of colonialism. He did not accept that Europeans went to Africa in order to improve life for the African people. They went, he said, primarily to make themselves rich. Colonialists were like robbers taking what did not belong to them. They had divided most of Africa between them, and treated the African people like servants. This state of affairs must be ended. Colonial peoples must work together to free themselves. For until they were free to govern themselves they would remain poor and unhappy. He ended the book:

'Peoples of the colonies unite : the working men of all countries are behind you.'

Nkrumah was thousands of miles away from home while he was in America. Yet he did not feel lonely. This was because there are millions of African people living in the USA. They are the descendants of Africans who were taken by force from their homes in Africa hundreds of years ago, and sold to work as slaves in America and the West Indies. Slavery was abolished in America in 1865. Then began the long, hard struggle of African Americans to obtain the same basic freedoms as white Americans.

Nkrumah was very interested in their struggle, and did all he could to assist them. He helped to set up an African Studies department in Lincoln. Soon afterwards, he began to organise the African Students' Association of America and Canada, and became its president. He welcomed into the Association not only students but Africans doing all kinds of other work. Soon the Association had a newspaper of its own, called the *African Interpreter*.

Everywhere he went in America, Nkrumah noticed that black Americans seemed to be having a very hard time. They lived in the worst houses, and only a very few seemed to obtain really good jobs. It saddened him to see Africans suffering because they belonged to a different race, and were not considered to be equals of white Americans. In some parts of America, Africans were not allowed to ride in the same buses as white people; and African children had to go to separate schools.

On one occasion, Nkrumah was refused a glass of water in a café because he was an African. The white waiter told him to go outside and drink from the tap in the yard.

This experience made Nkrumah more determined than ever to free Africa from foreign rule. For he believed that when Africa is free, then Africans, wherever they live, will be respected and able to improve their living conditions.

'Self-government is not an end in itself,' he said. 'It is a means to an end, to the building of the good life to the benefit of all.'

In May 1945, Nkrumah left America and went to England. He became a student of the London School of Economics where he studied law and economics. But he spent most of his time in political work.

There was in London at that time a students' organisation known as the West African Students' Union. Nkrumah joined it, and soon became vice-president. At meetings of the Union, members discussed the problems facing Africans both at home and abroad. They worked and planned to solve them.

Shortly after he arrived in London, Nkrumah helped a West Indian friend, George Padmore, to organise an important conference, known as the Fifth Pan-African Congress. This was held in Manchester in October 1945. Over 200 people from all over Africa and from other parts of the world attended. Their purpose was to link up all the various groups and movements seeking to end colonial rule, and to work out the best ways to achieve this goal. Members of the four previous Pan-African Congresses were mostly teachers, lawyers and so on, from the USA and the West Indies. But the Fifth Pan-African Congress was different. It contained students and workers, and most of the delegates came from Africa.

Nkrumah wrote a 'Declaration to the Colonial Peoples of the World' which members of the Congress approved. The Declaration began:

'We believe in the rights of all peoples to govern themselves. . . . The peoples of the colonies must have the right to elect their own government, a government without restrictions from a foreign power. We say to the peoples of the colonies that they must strive for these ends by all means at their disposal.'

It ended: 'Colonial and subject peoples of the world, unite.'

Soon after the Congress ended, Nkrumah and his friends formed the West African National Secretariat. Nkrumah was secretary. The purpose of the organisation was to plan for the independence of Africa. Nkrumah soon started a newspaper to make the work of the Secretariat known. He called the paper *The New African*. It sold very well. But it cost so much to produce that after a few months it had to be stopped.

The office was a small room near the centre of London. Nkrumah used to work there most of the time. During the cold weather it was difficult to keep the room warm because they could not get enough coal to keep the fire burning. Nkrumah would walk the streets of London looking for lumps of coal which had dropped off coal carts.

Nkrumah was just as short of money in London as he had been in America. He had scarcely enough for his lodgings, a tiny room which he rented for a small sum. Often Nkrumah and those who worked with him did not have enough to eat. So Nkrumah used to go round the dustbins of hotels and cafés to look for food. Sometimes he found fish heads. He would take them back to the office and make a fish stew for himself and his friends.

It was part of Nkrumah's work as vice-president of the West African Students' Union to try to help solve the many problems of students and workers. Some of them had difficulty in finding lodgings, or were worried about money and jobs. Sometimes there was trouble with the police. Nkrumah would attend law courts and visit prisons to help solve the problems. Although he was very busy he would always find time to listen to anyone who asked for his advice or help.

He joined the Coloured Workers' Association, an organisation set up to improve the working and living conditions of non-white workers in Britain. In order to help these people, Nkrumah travelled many hundreds of miles, visiting them at their work and in their homes.

Although Nkrumah already belonged to several organisations, he thought the time had come to form a special group from the most active members of the West African National Secretariat. The group was called *The Circle*. Members were sworn to secrecy, and promised 'to serve, sacrifice and suffer anything for the cause for which *The Circle* stands'. This meant that they would work with all their strength for the freedom of Africans to govern themselves, and for the unity of West Africa. This would be the first step in the unification of the entire continent of Africa.

Not long after *The Circle* was formed, Nkrumah received an invitation to return to the Gold Coast. It came from the United Gold

Coast Convention (UGCC), an organisation formed mainly by lawyers, doctors and chiefs, to end British colonial rule in the Gold Coast in the shortest possible time. They had heard about Nkrumah's work in London and wanted him to become general secretary of the UGCC.

Nkrumah hesitated. He had not finished his studies at the London School of Economics. But more important, he did not think that he would be able to work for long with the leaders of the UGCC. However, he eventually decided to go.

Before he left, he called a meeting of students and workers to tell them of his decision and to say goodbye. Many of them tried to persuade him not to go. But Nkrumah told them that the time had come to carry on their struggle on the soil of Africa. He said that he would never forget them, nor let them down.

On 14 November 1947, he left England on board a ship called the *Accra*. He was returning home at last after an absence of twelve years.

3 : Return to the Gold Coast. The struggle for self-government and the formation of the CPP

On his way home, Nkrumah visited Sierra Leone and Liberia. At that time, Sierra Leone was a British colony. But Liberia had been an independent state since 1847, when Africans who had been living as slaves in America and the West Indies went there to live. Africa was their home and they could live there as free men.

In Freetown, the capital of Sierra Leone, Nkrumah met an old friend named Wallace Johnson. The two had first met many years before in the Gold Coast. They had met again in London, and had worked together in the West African National Secretariat.

Wallace Johnson arranged for Nkrumah to speak at mass meetings in Freetown and at Fourah Bay College, the famous university of Sierra Leone. Nkrumah urged the students to organise for the hard struggle which lay ahead to end all forms of injustice and suffering. For it would be useless to chase out the colonial rulers if the Africans who replaced them were just as greedy and ruthless.

The ship called next at Monrovia, the capital city of Liberia, and once again Nkrumah went ashore. It was an exciting experience because it was the first time he had set foot in an independent African state. But he was disappointed to see that self-government had not brought much improvement in the lives of the ordinary people. Foreign businessmen, however, seemed to be making a lot of money. They were paying the Africans who worked for them very low wages, and were sending most of the money they made from Liberia's huge rubber plantations back to their home countries.

A few days after leaving Liberia, the ship docked at Takoradi,

With Nyaniba at Tarkwa after Nkrumah's return to the Gold Coast
in 1947

and Nkrumah was home again. The first thing he did was to go to
Tarkwa to see his mother. They had not seen each other for twelve
years and both had changed. Nyaniba's hair had turned white and
she was almost blind. Nkrumah had left as a student. He was now at
thirty-eight a mature, well-qualified man with much experience of
political work. Nyaniba hugged her son. They then drew up chairs
and began to tell each other all about what had happened since they
parted.

After a brief rest in Tarkwa, Nkrumah went to Saltpond. There he
met leading members of the UGCC, and set up an office for the
organisation. Within a few weeks he had drawn up a plan of campaign which he put before the Working Committee. In brief, the plan
was to link up with the UGCC existing organisations within the Gold

Coast, such as the trade unions, co-operative societies, farmers, women's and youth organisations. This would greatly strengthen the movement by broadening the membership. In addition, Nkrumah suggested the opening up of branches of the UGCC in every town and village. The Working Committee approved the plan of campaign, and supplied Nkrumah with an old car so that he could travel to every part of the country.

When Nkrumah began his work as general secretary of the UGCC only two branches existed. Within six months Nkrumah had succeeded in opening over five hundred branches. Day after day, week after week, he travelled long distances visiting every region of the country. At each village and town he explained the aims of the UGCC to the people and helped them to open a branch office. Many of the roads on which he travelled were no more than bumpy tracks, and Nkrumah's old car often broke down. Then he had to end his journey on foot. But sometimes he was too far from a village, and he had to wait by the roadside until he could get a lift in a passing lorry.

The British colonial rulers watched the rapid growth of the independence movement with alarm. While they were prepared to allow gradual political improvement they still maintained that the people of the Gold Coast were not ready to rule themselves.

The target of the UGCC was self-government in the 'shortest possible time'. The British did not mind this because they thought it meant that the UGCC would proceed peacefully step by step and would not press for immediate political change. But the whole position altered when Nkrumah began to call upon the people to demand self-government 'now'.

'The best way of learning to be an independent sovereign state', he said, 'is to be an independent sovereign state.'

It made him very angry to hear colonialists saying that Africans were not educated enough to govern themselves.

'What right has any colonial power to expect Africans to become "Europeans" or to have 100 per cent literacy before it considers them "ripe" for self-government? Wasn't the African, who is now considered "unprepared" to govern himself, governing himself before the advent of Europeans?'

Everywhere he went thousands gathered to hear him speak. At a mass meeting in Accra in February 1948, Dr Danquah, one of the founders of the UGCC, in supporting Nkrumah's speech, declared:

'Kwame Nkrumah will never fail you.'

'Freedom, freedom,' the people shouted.

Smiling and waving to them, Nkrumah replied:

'Self government *NOW*.'

'Self government *NOW*,' the crowd roared back.

It was not long before two events led to the outbreak of violence. First, a chief named Nii Kwabena Bonne called on the people to refuse to buy any goods from foreign shops. He said the prices were too high, and the people should show that they could manage without foreign goods. The people did as he asked and boycotted foreign shops. The boycott lasted for about a month. Then on the very day the boycott ended, the police opened fire on ex-servicemen who were peacefully marching to Christiansborg Castle to present a petition to the Governor. Two ex-servicemen were killed and five wounded.

News of the shooting quickly spread throughout Accra, and soon the town was in uproar. Angry crowds smashed their way into shops and houses owned by foreigners. Buildings and cars were set on fire. The rioting and looting lasted for several hours. As a result, some 29 people died and 237 were injured.

The colonial government blamed the UGCC, and particularly Nkrumah for the violence although he was not in Accra at the time. Police officers were sent to arrest him and five other leaders of the UGCC. The prisoners were flown to the far north of the country where they were detained for six weeks. In the meantime, the Governor set up a Commission of Enquiry under the chairmanship of Aiken Watson to investigate the causes of the disturbances and to make a report. Nkrumah and the other prisoners were brought to Accra to appear before the commissioners. Each prisoner was questioned separately. When the Watson Commissioners published their report in June 1948, they said that they considered Nkrumah largely to blame for the trouble because the UGCC 'did not really get down to business until the arrival of Mr Nkrumah on 16 December 1947'.

They recommended that changes should be made in the way the Gold
Coast was ruled to allow Africans to have a share in government.

As a result, the Governor named forty people to form a committee
under the chairmanship of a Ghanaian judge, Sir Henley Coussey.
This committee which came to be known as the Coussey Committee,
was to draw up a new plan of government for the Gold Coast. But
at the outset many thought it would not succeed because there was no
one on the committee to say what the ordinary people wanted. All
the members of the committee were big men – doctors, lawyers,
judges, and so on.

Nkrumah decided that the time had come to start a newspaper so
that the people could be informed of what was going on. With the
help of friends he bought a small printing machine, and on 3 September 1948 the first edition of his newspaper, the *Accra Evening News*
appeared. It was a great success. People rushed to buy it, and every
copy was quickly sold. As the days passed, many more people read it.
Large crowds used to gather outside the printing office to grab copies
as soon as they came off the press. Soon everyone knew the famous
mottoes which always appeared at the top of the front page:

We prefer self-government with danger to servitude in tranquillity
We have the right to live as men
We have the right to govern ourselves

Through the columns of the newspaper, Nkrumah urged the people
to keep up the pressure on the colonial power until victory was
achieved. In writing about the Coussey Committee he said that if its
report was unsatisfactory then he would declare 'Positive Action'. By
this he meant that the people would be called upon to adopt all kinds
of methods to show the colonial power that they would not accept the
report. They would go on strike, call boycotts, hold meetings and
demonstrations, and refuse to obey government orders.

For some time, there had been disagreement between Nkrumah
and the leaders of the UGCC. They thought he was pushing ahead
too fast in demanding self-government 'now'. Furthermore, they did
not like his talk of 'Positive Action'. They preferred slower and more

gradual change. They wanted an end to colonial rule mainly so that they could govern the country instead of the colonialists. But they did not want to see great changes in the lives of the ordinary working people. They feared that Nkrumah, as the champion of the masses, was aiming at something quite different. He was bringing the workers and the young people strongly into the movement. For he regarded self-government as only a first step in the total liberation of the people from all forms of injustice. He wanted to work for a new Ghana in which everyone would have a fair chance.

The young people who supported Nkrumah were members of the Committee on Youth Organisation (CYO). The CYO, formed largely as a result of Nkrumah's efforts, was to be the youth section of the UGCC. But leaders of the UGCC distrusted the CYO because the members were mainly from the poorer sections of the population. The CYO, like Nkrumah, aimed to build a Ghana in which there would be no people with special privileges.

By mid-1949 it had become clear that Nkrumah and the CYO could no longer continue to work within the UGCC. They wanted different things. They decided, therefore, to form a new party to be known as the Convention People's Party (CPP). The CPP was launched by Nkrumah before a crowd of about 60,000 people in the Arena in Accra on 12 June 1949.

'The time has arrived', he said, 'when a definite line of action must be taken if we are going to save our country from continued imperialist exploitation and oppression. . . . I am happy to be able to tell you that the CYO, owing to the present political tension, has decided to transform itself into a fully-fledged political party with the object of promoting the fight for full self-government now.'

He went on to tell them that the party aimed to build a 'better Ghana' in which everyone 'shall have the right to live and govern themselves as free people'. The motto of the CPP would be:

FORWARD EVER – BACKWARD NEVER

4 : Positive action and imprisonment

There were soon branches of the CPP in every town and village. The people supported the new party because they felt it really belonged to them. It had been formed by them, and for them. They had become tired of listening to leaders of the UGCC telling them to be patient. How could they continue to be patient when every day they saw foreigners using the land and the labour of Ghanaians to enrich themselves?

The people of Ghana through the CPP demanded that the British grant self-government at once. Ghanaians had managed their own affairs before the arrival of colonialists. They would do so again.

The CPP flag coloured red, white and green, flew from wooden poles in almost every village. At party meetings the people gave the CPP freedom sign raising their right hands and shouting 'Victory'. After discussing party business, men, women and children would often join in singing the party song:

> There is victory for us
> There is victory for us
> In the struggle of the CPP
> There is victory for us.
>
> For us, for us, for us,
> In the struggle of the CPP
> There is victory for us.

Nkrumah had warned that if the Report of the Coussey Committee was unsatisfactory, then he would call for Positive Action. The Report was published at the end of October 1949. It provided for

Africans to have more say in how Ghana was governed. But the real power was still to remain with the colonial Governor.

Nkrumah at once called a meeting of people from all parts of Ghana to study the Report and to decide what to do. The gathering was known as the Ghana People's Representative Assembly. Members of the Assembly agreed that the Coussey Report was unacceptable and declared that the people of Ghana would themselves decide how they wished to be governed. A note was sent to the Governor informing him of the Assembly's decision, warning him that Positive Action would be taken if the British continued to deny Ghanaians the right to govern themselves.

Nkrumah said that he would give the colonial government two weeks in which to call an Assembly of the Ghanaian people to draw up plans for a new constitution. If at the end of two weeks this had not been done, he would proclaim the start of Positive Action.

The Colonial Secretary tried to persuade Nkrumah to give up his plan for Positive Action. He warned Nkrumah that he would be held personally responsible if any violence broke out.

Two weeks passed, and still the British government refused to agree to the demands of the Ghana People's Representative Assembly. Therefore, on 8 January 1950, Nkrumah declared the start of Positive Action. At a huge meeting at the Arena in Accra he called on all workers, except those employed in hospitals and in other essential services, to stop work at midnight.

He then rushed off to declare Positive Action in Cape Coast, Sekondi and Tarkwa. All over Ghana people refused to work. Shops, offices and factories closed. Trains and buses were at a standstill.

The colonial government was frightened. It stopped all public meetings, and ordered the police to break into offices of the CPP to arrest key members of the party. The office of Nkrumah's newspaper, the *Accra Evening News*, was raided and closed down. By then, most of the CPP leaders throughout the country had been imprisoned. Nkrumah was one of the last to be arrested.

As he was driven in a police van to James Fort prison in Accra on 22 January 1950, he heard on the car radio the announcement of his capture:

'Kwame Nkrumah was arrested early this morning. There was no trouble, and all was quiet at the scene of arrest.'

The news bulletin was repeated several times. For the colonial government wanted to be sure that everyone would hear the news that the CPP leader, Kwame Nkrumah, had been imprisoned. The government thought there would then be no further trouble. For with Nkrumah and most of the other CPP leaders in prison, they thought the people would go back to work and in time forget about the independence struggle.

The colonial government was wrong. The imprisonment of Nkrumah, and the attempt to suppress the CPP, only strengthened the people's determination to end colonial rule. Frequently, large crowds collected outside James Fort to sing hymns and party songs to let the prisoners know that they were not forgotten.

Conditions in the prison were very bad. The food was poor and there was not enough of it. Nkrumah shared a small cell with ten others. They had to sleep on the floor, and to use a bucket in a corner of the cell as a latrine.

Nkrumah at once set to work to organise the CPP prisoners into a committee. He told his comrades that they must prepare party plans for the general election due to take place in February 1951. The CPP, he said, must win the election. In order to do this, there must be a CPP candidate in every part of Ghana.

'I myself will stand for Accra Central,' he said.

At first some of his comrades thought he was joking. How could he, a prisoner, hope to be elected? They did not know that every night after they were asleep he was hard at work. A lamp in the street outside the prison made a small circle of light on the floor of the cell. Nkrumah was able to use the patch of light to write messages to party members outside. One night he wrote fifty sheets of instructions. He wrote on lavatory paper which he obtained from other prisoners in exchange for some of his food ration. The messages were given to a friendly warder who smuggled them out of the prison and delivered them to party headquarters. The warder returned with letters telling Nkrumah all the latest news.

On election day there was great excitement in James Fort. The prisoners knew that Nkrumah was standing for Accra Central and they all wanted him to win. Even the prison governor was interested, and he allowed Nkrumah to be given hourly reports on how the election was going. As the results began to be announced it became increasingly clear that the CPP was likely to be victorious. But it was not until early morning on the next day that Nkrumah was told that he had been elected. He had obtained 22,780 votes out of 23,122. This was the largest number of votes anyone had ever before polled in the history of the country.

The prisoners in James Fort and the people of Ghana were jubilant. Crowds collected in the streets of Accra to celebrate, and the police had difficulty in stopping them from marching to James Fort to demand Nkrumah's release.

The CPP had won such a great victory in the general election that the colonial Governor was compelled to agree to free Nkrumah. But the actual time of his release was to be kept secret because the Governor feared it might be impossible to control the excited crowds.

Nkrumah's journey from prison to CPP headquarters in Accra,
12 February 1951

About midday on 12 February 1951, the prison gates of James Fort were opened. Out stepped Kwame Nkrumah a free man after over a year in prison. News of his imminent release had leaked out and crowds had gathered to greet him. They cheered and pushed forward as he appeared. Everyone wanted to catch a glimpse of their leader and to shake him by the hand. For a moment it seemed as if Nkrumah might be crushed as the crowd surged forward. But soon he was being carried shoulder-high to the car waiting to take him to party headquarters.

5 : Ghana is born

The day after Nkrumah left prison the colonial Governor invited him to Christiansborg Castle, his official residence. Everyone knew the reason. The Governor was going to ask him to form a government.

As Nkrumah entered the massive, white stone castle the Governor hurried forward to greet him. He was curious to meet the fearless Ghanaian whom he had heard so much about. After congratulating Nkrumah on the CPP victory in the general election the Governor said that Nkrumah should become Leader of Government Business. He asked Nkrumah to choose seven party members to become cabinet ministers. But the Governor made it clear that he himself would continue to be head of the cabinet. In addition, the Governor would appoint three British cabinet ministers to be in charge of the important ministries of foreign affairs, finance and justice.

Nkrumah wanted the government of Ghana to be entirely in African hands. But he knew this could not be achieved immediately. He therefore agreed to discuss the Governor's proposals with party members.

On leaving the castle, Nkrumah went straight to party headquarters and for many hours discussed the situation with members of the central committee. If members of the CPP took part in government they would be in a stronger position to work towards self-government. They would also gain valuable experience of the work of government. The committee therefore decided the CPP should co-operate.

Soon afterwards, Nkrumah called all CPP members of the National Assembly to a meeting. He told them that although the party had agreed to share in the work of government this did not mean that they were satisfied with the arrangement. It was only a temporary agreement, and a first step on the road to full self-government. They must not relax for one moment until Ghana had been completely freed from colonial rule. He reminded them that colonial governments never gave independence to a colony until forced to do so. For freedom is not something which is given to a people simply because they ask for it. It is won only as a result of struggle and sacrifice.

'I know of no case', he said, 'where self-government has been handed to a people on a silver platter. The dynamic has had to come from the people themselves.' He went on to warn them of the dangers which might face them in their new positions of responsibility. People might try to bribe them to gain special favours. Members of the Assembly might become proud and forget that they owed their success to the people who had elected them. Or they might be tempted to build large houses, and spend a lot of money on cars, clothes and expensive food. Members should always remember the trust which the people had placed in them. This was the most precious thing they possessed. Without the support of the people they were nothing.

'The spirit of Positive Action', he declared, 'has made the party what it is today and Positive Action must maintain it.' He ended: 'The exploited and oppressed people of colonial Africa and elsewhere are looking up to us for hope and inspiration. . . . The torch of the liberation movement has been lifted up in Ghana for the whole of West Africa, and it will blaze a trail of freedom for other oppressed territories.'

Nkrumah was given an office and a small staff to help him. There was so much government and party work to do that he was seldom able to rest for more than a few hours each night. Usually he got up at four in the morning. He would then go through his papers and prepare for the day's work ahead. Often before he had finished, people would begin arriving to discuss various matters with him. Some simply wanted advice on a family difficulty. Others wanted to tell Nkrumah about troublesome problems concerning their work. They knew that he was interested in every problem, however small, and that he would do his best to help them. But most of the people who visited Nkrumah at that time wanted to hear him talk about the plans to achieve full self-government for the people of Ghana. It made them very happy to hear him speak of the day when the colonialists would leave Ghana, never to return. Ghanaians would then be free to get on with the hard work of developing their country in the way they wished.

There was so much to do. During the long years of colonial rule the British had been mainly concerned with getting gold, diamonds and cocoa out of the country to enrich themselves. They had spent little time or money on making improvements for the people of Ghana. So in 1951, when the CPP first took part in government, the country was in a very poor state. There were only a few roads, and hardly any railways. Most of the villages had no piped water supply or electricity. The farmers of Ghana needed modern farm machinery; and large areas of good farming country remained uncultivated. In the towns, many people lived in dirty and overcrowded huts. They did not have enough to eat, and some of them suffered from terrible diseases. Hundreds of thousands of Ghanaians did not know how to read or write. The soil of Ghana produced many things which could be used for making goods which Ghanaians needed, yet there were no industries.

The CPP were determined to change all that. More and better houses would be built. There would be new roads and railways, schools, hospitals, factories, offices and shops. No Ghanaian would need to go hungry or to lack work. All Ghanaian children would be able to go to school because the government would pay the fees. There was plenty for everyone's needs to be satisfied if the people worked hard and unselfishly.

A start could be made to put the plans into operation, but Nkrumah warned that progress would be slow until Ghana was completely free from colonial rule. It is only when a people are free that they can fully carry out their plans.

'Seek first the political kingdom', he said, 'and all else will follow.'

It was not easy for the CPP to share the work of government with the colonial power. The people who worked in government offices, the civil servants, had been used to taking orders from the British, and some of them did not like Ghanaians telling them what to do. To show their dislike, some of the top civil servants were deliberately slow in carrying out an order, or pretended that they had never received it. In this way they hoped to prolong colonial rule. There was trouble also among certain officers in the army and the police. These men were mostly British and they found it difficult to accept the changes that were taking place in Ghana. In addition, the three cabinet ministers chosen by the Governor controlled the key ministries of foreign affairs, finance and justice, and therefore held the real power in the cabinet. Ghanaians were given the less important ministries of education, social welfare, mines, communications and local government. Furthermore, the Governor had the power to stop any laws from being passed if he did not like them. He could, if he wished, even prevent the National Assembly from meeting.

On 5 March 1952, Nkrumah became prime minister. He was the first African ever to hold this position. By then, the CPP had begun the task of setting up a Ghanaian civil service. All civil servants from overseas were given the choice of either leaving Ghana or of becoming members of the new civil service. Many remained, but some took the money offered to them to compensate them for the loss of their jobs, and returned home. For a time there were not enough trained Ghanaian civil servants to fill all the vacancies.

There were similar problems when it came to replacing colonial army and police officers with Ghanaians. This could not be done immediately. But the process was begun, and gradually more and more Ghanaians took over top positions in the civil service, army and police. Nkrumah allowed any European who wanted to stay and work in Ghana to do so. But they had to be prepared to work entirely for Ghana, and not to have feelings of loyalty towards the British government.

Nkrumah was never against any person simply because he belonged to another race. He judged people according to their ability and their work. If they could do some useful work, and were prepared to serve the people, then a place could be found for them. It did not matter which country they came from.

On 10 July 1953, less than two years after the 1951 election, Nkrumah made one of the most important speeches of his life. It was

called the 'Motion of Destiny'. In this speech, made in the National
Assembly in Accra, Nkrumah demanded that the British government
proclaim an early date for Ghana's full independence.

'Our demand for self-government is a just demand,' he said. 'It is a
demand admitting of no compromise. The right of a people to govern
themselves is a fundamental principle, and to compromise on this
principle is to betray it.'

He spoke of the long struggle of the people of Ghana to regain their
freedom. He said that the CPP had only agreed to take part in
government after the 1951 election in order to be in a better position
to work for self-government. 'We can never rest satisfied with what
we have so far achieved. . . . Our country has proved that it is more
than ready.' He reminded members of the Assembly of the great West
African empire which before the eleventh century stretched from
Timbuktu to Bamako and beyond. At that time Britain was a poor
and very unimportant country, while Ghana was strong and wealthy.

'It is said that lawyers and scholars were much respected in that
empire and that the inhabitants of Ghana wore garments of wool,
cotton, silk and velvet. There was trade in copper, gold and textile
fabrics; and jewels and weapons of gold were carried. Thus we may
take pride in the name of Ghana,' Nkrumah said. 'What our
ancestors achieved . . . gives us confidence that we can create, out of
that past, a glorious future, not in the terms of war and military
pomp, but in terms of social progress and peace.'

Nkrumah then proposed changes in the existing Coussey
constitution to give Ghanaians a greater share in the government of
the country. One of the reforms he called for was an increase in
the number of members of the National Assembly. In addition, he
wanted all members of the cabinet to be members of the Assembly.
This would mean getting rid of the three members chosen by the
Governor and replacing them with Ghanaians.

It was a long speech but no one noticed the time passing. All were
listening intently to what Nkrumah had to say. When he finished
speaking, members jumped to their feet. They cheered, clapped and
sang the party song. They made such a noise that the crowds waiting
in the street outside heard, and they too began to cheer.

Members of the Assembly discussed the Motion of Destiny for the next two days. Then everyone voted for it. The Governor thereupon declared that another general election would be held for the people to choose members to occupy the extra seats in the Assembly, and to show if they supported the Motion of Destiny.

As the time for the election drew near, Nkrumah visited every part of Ghana to explain to the people the importance of their vote. 'This is your chance,' he told them. 'This is what we have been planning for, suffering for, slaving for. The fulfilment of our promise of "Freedom Now" is at hand.' Everywhere he went the people stopped what they were doing and hurried to hear him speak.

On 15 June 1954, the day of the election, all the excitement seemed over as the people went quietly to vote. But in the evening, as the votes were being counted, and the results began to be declared, people rushed out to celebrate. For it was soon clear that the CPP was going to win another election victory.

When all the votes had been counted the CPP had won 72 out of the 104 seats in the Assembly. Of the other seats, 12 were won by the Northern Peoples' Party, and 20 by people who called themselves 'Independents' because they did not belong to any party.

The next day, the Governor asked Nkrumah to form a government. But this time all members of the cabinet were to be members of the CPP. The new government was quickly formed, and once again Nkrumah led the campaign for immediate self-government. But there was at this time a small group of selfish people who did not want the CPP to lead the country to independence. These people wanted Ghana to be divided into separate regions with each region managing its own affairs.

Such an arrangement would greatly weaken the central government in Accra. It was not sensible to split up the government of a country as small as Ghana. Again and again Nkrumah tried to persuade those who opposed the CPP to meet and discuss their problems with him, but they refused. Instead, they did all they could to cause trouble so that the British would think the Ghanaian people were not ready for independence. They tried to break up CPP meetings, and attacked members of the CPP. One of them placed a bomb in the yard outside Nkrumah's house in Accra. Luckily no one was injured when it exploded. But all the windows in the house were broken.

Because of the actions of this small group of people the British government said that there must be another general election in Ghana to show definitely that the people of Ghana wished the CPP to lead them to independence. The date of the election was fixed for 17 July 1956.

Once again the CPP won a clear victory. Yet Kofi Busia, one of the leaders of those who opposed the CPP, flew to London to try to stop the British government from granting independence to Ghana. Fortunately for Ghana he did not succeed.

On the eve of independence, thousands of people crowded into the Accra arena to witness the ceremony marking the end of colonial rule. It was exactly at 12 o'clock, midnight, that the British flag was taken down. One minute later, on 6 March 1957, the new flag of Ghana was raised in its place. Then, as soon as his voice could be heard amid the cheering, Nkrumah proclaimed that Ghana was free and independent at last.

The first stage of the struggle was over. Ghanaians were free to govern themselves. But harder struggles lay ahead. In the words of Nkrumah: 'The African in every part of this vast continent has been awakened and the struggle for freedom will go on. It is our duty to offer what assistance we can to those now engaged in the battles which we ourselves have fought and won. Our task is not done and our safety not assured until the last vestiges of colonialism have been swept from Africa.'

6: 'Africa must be free. Africa must be united.'

In 1957, when colonial rule ended in Ghana, there were only eight independent African states. They were Ghana, Ethiopia, Libya, Tunisia, Morocco, Egypt, Liberia and Sudan. Most of the African people were still unfree to govern themselves. They were ruled either by colonial governments or by people of European descent who had settled in Africa.

Nkrumah believed it to be the duty of all who had obtained their freedom to work together to help those still struggling to be free. He therefore invited members of the governments of each of the independent states to meet in Accra in April 1958. It was the first Conference of Independent African States ever to be held.

Most of the members of the conference lived in the northern part of Africa. In welcoming them to Ghana, Nkrumah said: 'Today we are one. If in the past the Sahara divided us, now it unites us.' By this he meant that they no longer had to live separated from one another as in colonial times.

In their grab for colonies the colonial powers had divided the land of Africa between them creating artificial boundaries between African peoples. When colonial rule ended Africans were free to disregard the old colonial frontiers, and to pursue Pan-African policies by working together as one people.

'In meeting Africans from all parts of the continent', Nkrumah said, 'I am constantly impressed by how much we have in common. It is not just our colonial past, or the fact that we have aims in common, it is something which goes far deeper. I can best describe it as a sense of oneness in that we are *Africans*.'

Ghana, Egypt and Sudan had been colonised by the British; Libya and Ethiopia by the Italians; Morocco by the French; and Liberia by the American Colonisation Society. Now that they were free, each of the governments of the independent states faced much the same problems. All wished to bring about a rapid and big improvement in the living conditions of their people, and to help in the liberation of the rest of Africa.

Members of the conference discussed ways to achieve these aims. They agreed that they must keep in closer touch so that they could help one another. To do this it would be necessary to build new roads and railways; to improve air services; to extend telephone and postal links. For colonial governments had done very little to provide communications between African states. Most of the colonial roads and railways were built to enable goods from the mines, plantations and forests of Africa to be taken to the ports for shipment overseas.

There was very little trade between African states. The main concern of colonialists had been to provide good links with Europe. For example, it was still easier for a person wishing to travel from Nairobi to Accra to fly first to a European airport, and to get a connection to Accra from there.

Six weeks after the conference ended, Nkrumah visited all the countries which had taken part. He wanted to see for himself how they were getting on. But more important, he wished to plan with them how to speed up the work of liberating and unifying Africa.

An important first step towards African unification was taken in December 1958, when Nkrumah and his great friend Sékou Touré of the Republic of Guinea signed an agreement to unite their countries. They hoped that the Ghana–Guinea Union would encourage other African states to follow their example. In April 1961, the Republic of Mali joined and the Ghana–Guinea–Mali Union was formed. At that time, Modibo Keita was president of Mali.

Both Guinea and Mali had been colonies of France. They were therefore different in many ways from Ghana which had been a British colony. Sékou Touré and Modibo Keita spoke French. Nkrumah spoke English. But the three leaders had the same ideas

about freedom and unity. As Nkrumah said: 'The forces making for
unity far outweigh those which divide us.'

Before the Ghana–Guinea Union was formed, Nkrumah had
arranged for the calling of an All-African Peoples' Conference.
Members of freedom movements and other peoples' organisations
from all over Africa were invited to attend. Although there had been
five previous Pan-African conferences this was the first to be held in
Africa. Nkrumah had done one of the things he said he would do.
He had taken the Pan-African movement to Africa, its true home.

The people of Accra gave the conference members a big welcome.
They decorated the city with flags, and thousands went to the airport
to cheer and wave as each delegate arrived. Some Ghanaians carried
placards proclaiming:

HANDS OFF AFRICA
AFRICA MUST BE
FREE

Heads of state of the Ghana–Guinea–Mali Union formed in 1961. From
left to right, Sékou Touré, Modibo Keita, Kwame Nkrumah

These same words were written in large letters above the platform in the conference hall.

A special archway was built leading to the Community Centre where the conference was held. Below the words: ALL AFRICAN PEOPLES' CONFERENCE was a map of Africa with a flaming torch drawn across it. This was the torch of African freedom which Nkrumah had lit at Ghana's independence in 1957. He said it would continue to burn until the whole of Africa was free.

Over 300 people attended the conference. Among them were Patrice Lumumba and Frantz Fanon, and many other leaders of freedom movements in their own countries. Lumumba became the first prime minister of Zaire when the country became independent in 1960. Zaire had previously been a colony of Belgium.

Frantz Fanon was a West Indian doctor who had resolved to devote his life to helping the people of Algeria to free themselves from French colonial rule. He was a member of the Front for National Liberation (FLN), the Algerian people's movement which fought the French and successfully won independence for Algeria in 1962.

Members of the conference told each other about their difficulties, and discussed ways to overcome them. Each felt very encouraged to know that others were engaged in a similar struggle to free their countries from foreign rule. They agreed they must use peaceful methods as far as possible, but that if these failed to bring results then they must be prepared to fight.

When Fanon spoke about the war in Algeria, everyone listened very carefully to what he had to say. For they knew that the time was not far off when the people of their countries might also have to take up arms.

By the end of the conference some very important questions had been decided. It was agreed that freedom fighters should be helped with supplies of all kinds, and that training camps should be set up for them in liberated areas. Nkrumah suggested that an army should be formed of volunteers from all over Africa, so that every African could help in the freedom struggle.

Soon after the conference ended, freedom fighters from all over Africa began to arrive in Ghana. Nkrumah arranged for camps to be set up for them where they could organise and train. Ghana became known as a place where anyone fighting against colonialism or any other injustice could be sure of encouragement and support. Nkrumah himself would spend hours discussing problems with them. Always he advised them to work closely together. Any differences between them could be settled once they had freed their countries. Meantime, all should join together to defeat the common enemy.

'In a few years from now', he said, 'we can envisage that all Africa will be free from colonial rule. Nothing can stem our onward march to independence and freedom.'

Gradually, the colonial powers were forced to give up more of their colonies in Africa. The year 1960 became known as 'Africa Year' because in that year colonial rule ended in such a large number of African states.

In most cases, the African people were able to obtain independence without fighting. They used methods of Positive Action similar to those used by the CPP in Ghana. For example, Nigeria, Sierra Leone, Gambia, Tanzania, Uganda and Zambia won their independence in this way. In other colonies, such as Algeria, Kenya, Ethiopia, Angola and Mozambique, the people had to fight for their freedom. In each case, the people only began armed struggle when it became clear that they could not free themselves in any other way.

By 1963, there were 32 independent African states. This was a great achievement. It was six years since Ghana had become independent and at that time there were only eight.

But most of the newly independent states seemed poor compared with countries in other parts of the world. This was mainly because they still suffered from the weakening effects of colonialism. Few of them could manage without support. It was therefore very important that they should help each other as much as possible. As it was, they were having to seek aid from outside Africa and this would become a danger to their independence if the aid was not freely given. No people can be truly independent if others control their industries and trade. Those who own the wealth of a country will by various means try to interfere in the way it is governed so that nothing is done to harm their interests. The country might seem to be free, but it is 'sham' independence because the people are not masters in their own house.

Nkrumah called this indirect form of rule 'neocolonialism'. He said: 'The essence of neocolonialism is that the state which is subject to it is, in theory, independent . . . In reality its economic system and thus its political policy is directed from outside.'

Again and again he warned that while Africa remained divided, no state could be secure or free to develop in the way it wished. Divided they were weak, but united they would be strong and able to plan the development of Africa as a whole for the good of all the African people. The richer states could help the poorer ones, and by working together everyone would benefit.

It is nonsense, he said, to talk of Africa being poor. Africa has plenty of everything. It is the second largest continent in the world, and has natural resources to make it one of the richest. It is the African people who are poor, and this is the result of centuries of colonialism.

'Africa must be free. Africa must be united.'

Nkrumah wrote a book called *Africa Must Unite*. This was published in 1963, just before the conference of 32 independent African states opened in Addis Ababa in May. Copies of the book were distributed to conference members. Also in front of them were proposals drawn up by Nkrumah for African unity.

'There is no time to waste', he wrote, 'for we must unite now or perish, since no single African state is large or powerful enough to stand on its own.'

The day the conference opened, Nkrumah made a long speech urging members to begin at once the task of unification :

'What is the alternative to this?' he asked. 'If we falter at this stage, and let time pass for neocolonialism to consolidate its position on this continent, what will be the fate of our people who have put their trust in us? What will be the fate of our freedom fighters? What will be the fate of other African territories that are not yet free?'

Nkrumah went on to propose the setting up of a Liberation Committee. All the independent states would pay money into it so that help could be given to freedom fighters. This would speed up the work of liberating the rest of Africa.

In Addis Ababa in 1963 when the Organisation of African Unity was
founded. Kwame Nkrumah is urging the member states to form an
All-African Union Government

Everyone supported the idea of African liberation and unity. But
they did not agree on how to proceed. Some, like the heads of state of
Ivory Coast and Senegal, wanted a very gradual approach to unification. They said the African states should concentrate on improving

trade with one another. Others, like Nkrumah and Sékou Touré, wanted members to declare there and then that they agreed to establish a union of African states. They believed that regional economic organisations would prove ineffective and would only hinder progress towards the political unification of Africa. The economy of Africa must be planned and developed on a continental scale through unified political machinery.

After much discussion it was decided to form the Organisation of African Unity (OAU). The charter of the OAU was signed in Addis Ababa on 25 May 1963 by the heads of 32 independent states. Its purpose was to work for the unity, freedom and prosperity of the people of Africa. Many committees were formed including a Liberation Committee. But no government machinery was set up to be the basis of a union government of Africa; and there was no means of enforcing OAU decisions.

The OAU was therefore not what Nkrumah wanted. But if all went well he thought it could be a beginning: 'We have proved at Addis Ababa', he said, 'that we are ready to build a united Africa.'

7 : Development plans

One evening, not long after independence, Nkrumah decided to go for a drive. He had been working hard all day in his office in Flagstaff House, and felt like a breath of sea air before the cabinet meeting. He called to the foreign visitor who was just leaving his office and asked him if he would like to go too.

Soon they were being driven through Accra towards the coastal road. It was already getting dark but the streets were filled with people. Some were hurrying home from work. Others seemed to be just strolling around, chatting and laughing with friends. Traders still sat at their stalls selling all kinds of things. Cars, taxis, lorries and buses blew their horns as they slowly forced their way through the crowds. It seemed such a busy, noisy place. Nkrumah was happy. He loved to be among the people, specially when no one noticed him.

Suddenly, he asked the driver to stop. They had left the town centre and were going along the quiet coastal road. A short distance away, on the narrow strip of grass between the road and the beach was a wooden bench beneath a single street lamp. Sitting there reading, and quite alone, was a schoolboy, about twelve years old.

'You see him?' Nkrumah asked the visitor sitting beside him. 'He is doing his homework. He has no light in his house.' He paused. 'Soon it will be possible for every house in Ghana to have electric light.'

He told the driver to proceed slowly so as not to disturb him, and as the car glided past the boy did not look up.

Long before independence, Nkrumah and his colleagues had been working out plans to improve living conditions for the people of Ghana. But they were not free to proceed as fast as they would like with their development plans until colonial rule ended. With independence in 1957, they were at last able to go ahead with all speed.

'Our natural resources are abundant and varied,' Nkrumah told the people. 'We have mineral and agricultural wealth and, above all, we have the will to find the means whereby these possessions can be put to the greatest use and advantage. The party's programme for work and happiness is a pointer to the way ahead, the way leading to a healthier and more prosperous life for us all.'

He was speaking on the radio to tell Ghanaians about the government's Seven Year Development Plan of 1964. He asked everyone to get a copy of the Plan and to send in any suggestions for improvements.

'The party will take no action on the programme until the masses of the people have had the fullest opportunity of reviewing it . . . Ghana is our country which we must all help to build . . . We have a gigantic task before us.'

The aim, he said, was to develop Ghana into a modern state in which everyone would have sufficient for their needs. This would mean building industries and producing new and different crops. Instead of working for colonialists, Ghanaians would be working for their own welfare and happiness and to make themselves strong enough to help in the liberation of the rest of Africa. They would develop the land and the natural resources of Ghana to the fullest extent for the benefit of all the people.

'There is a job', he said, 'for every man, woman and child.'

In colonial times there was not a single industry in Ghana, and the country had been dependent on selling one crop – cocoa. When the price of cocoa was high in world markets there was money to spend for buying from abroad some of the things Ghanaians needed. But when the price dropped, as it often did through no fault of the cocoa farmers, the whole country suffered.

Nkrumah and the CPP were determined to make Ghana more self-reliant. The more things they could grow, or make themselves, the less they would have to buy from overseas.

'I seek the active support, goodwill, and maximum effort of everyone in Ghana', he said, 'so that this great Plan can become a reality.

It will bring not only satisfaction and higher standards of living to our people, but will also serve as an inspiration to our brothers in other parts of this great continent who are still struggling to be free.'

He took no notice of those who argued that the conditions and resources of Africa were not suited to industrial development. Such people were trying to excuse the colonial powers for not building industries in Africa.

He said: 'We have in Africa everything necessary to become a powerful, modern, industrialised continent . . . Far from having inadequate resources, Africa is probably better equipped for industrialisation than almost any other region in the world.'

During the next nine years after independence, Ghanaians worked harder than they had ever done before to make the development plans a success. New houses, hospitals, schools, training colleges, factories, shops and offices were built. New roads and railways linked up all parts of Ghana. Ghana Airways was formed, and soon Ghanaian aircraft were flying on many new routes in Africa and elsewhere. Ghana also had her own shipping line, called the Black Star Line. There were soon factories making cloth, soap, shoes, cement, water storage tanks, glass, paint, chemicals, medicines, furniture and many other things which previously had to be imported.

Ghanaian farmers continued to produce cocoa. But using new farm machinery they also grew other crops, both to feed the people and to provide materials needed for the factories. Large areas were sown with cotton to be used to make cloth in the new textile mills. Thousands of rubber trees were planted to supply rubber for the motor tyre factory, and for selling overseas. On the fertile coastal plains, farmers grew cereals and vegetables, and increased their stock of chickens and cattle to provide a better diet for the people. In the far north of Ghana, tobacco, yams and rice were grown. Throughout the country the people were encouraged to grow more sugar cane, bananas, pineapples, coconuts, oranges, grapefruit, lemons and oil palms. By 1970 there were to be four factories producing enough sugar to supply all that Ghana needed.

Fishermen were provided with motor boats so that they could go to distant fishing grounds which they had been unable to reach in

Development Plans. Kwame Nkrumah inspecting progress of work on
Tema Harbour

their canoes. They caught more fish, and this made it possible for
supplies to be put in tins in the new canning factories. These factories
were built to preserve not only fish but also pineapple and other fruit
grown in Ghana.

Many of the factories were built at Tema, a new coastal town 18
miles east of Accra. In 1957 there was nothing there. Yet within six
years a modern town and one of the biggest man-made harbours in
Africa had been built at Tema. Apart from the factories, there were
houses, offices, schools, shops, markets, a hospital, playing areas and a
printing press. To link Tema with Accra was a wide motorway along
which cars and lorries could travel quickly and safely.

Nkrumah often used to see for himself how work was progressing
on the various development projects. One of the places he liked to
visit most was Akosombo, where the greatest of all Ghana's development projects was being built. This was the Volta dam which would,
when completed, be able to provide enough electricity for every

Ghanaian home, and for the new factories. There would also be plenty of electricity to spare.

'This project is not for Ghana alone,' Nkrumah declared. 'I have already offered to share our power resources with our sister African states.'

As a vast lake formed behind the dam, thousands of people had to be moved from their homes. They were given fresh land to farm, and modern houses which had electricity and a piped water supply. Schools and shops were built, and soon everyone settled down happily in the new villages.

Gradually, the Volta lake became a huge reservoir providing an improved water supply for towns and villages for hundreds of miles. All around, farmers dug trenches so that water from the lake could flow over land which had previously been too dry to farm.

The Volta River Project was completed sooner than expected because everyone worked so hard on it. At a special ceremony at Akosombo on 23 January 1966 Nkrumah switched on lights to signify that electricity had begun to flow from the Volta. One of his greatest dreams had come true. Ghana would be able to have all the electricity needed for her developing industries. She had at last the means to become a modern, industrialised country.

Work was started on the building of smaller dams and reservoirs in other parts of Ghana; and new wells were sunk in places where a piped water supply could not be provided. As each year passed, more and more Ghanaians were able to have all the water they needed.

Nkrumah had a small house built for himself high up on a hill overlooking the Volta dam. But he could not go there very often because he was too busy. Often he would have to travel abroad, but when he was in Accra he lived next to his office in Flagstaff House. He could have lived in Christiansborg Castle where the colonial Governor used to stay. But he preferred to live simply, and in a small place.

Every day he got up long before most people were awake, and he seldom went to bed before midnight. Very often it was one or two o'clock in the morning before he finished working. He slept for about four hours, and then he was up again. He would do exercises to keep fit, play tennis, or walk for several miles. For breakfast he liked to have the yolk of an egg or some fruit. Sometimes he had nothing except a fruit drink or a cup of tea. Then he would walk across to his office and work through until about 2.30, when he had a light lunch. If there was time he had a short rest before returning to the office to work without a break until late at night.

Sometimes when it was very dark, and he was walking back from his office he would hear the roar of lions. The lions were very close for they were in the grounds of Flagstaff House in the small zoo which Nkrumah had gradually built up over the years. He loved animals and birds and wanted to have as many as possible near to him. There were lions, ostriches, zebras, crocodiles, baboons, apes, giraffes, gazelles, and many other animals. There were all kinds of snakes, and many sorts of birds. Nkrumah knew them all, and whenever he had a few moments to spare he would walk round to see them. He was particularly happy when children visited the zoo. He knew they enjoyed seeing the animals as much as he did. He wanted the children to learn all about them, to understand their different needs, and how to treat them.

Once, when a number of zebras arrived late at night from East Africa, in big wooden cages, Nkrumah was angry because the man in charge was going to leave them in cages until the morning. The man was tired, and said that as the animals had been shut up for several weeks another night would not matter.

'All the more reason to release them now,' Nkrumah said. 'They have been caged long enough. I will not have them in cages for another night.'

The man had to set to work there and then to let them out and put them in the pleasant open space provided for them.

Some people thought that Nkrumah was always in too much of a hurry to get things done. He seemed to push ahead with new plans often before existing ones had been fully carried out. Nkrumah admitted that he was impatient when it came to rebuilding Ghana, and working for the freedom and happiness of the people of Africa. Africans, he said, could not afford to go at the pace of camels when other parts of the world were jet propelled.

'We are running against time in Africa,' he declared. 'Not only have we to eliminate or eradicate the deficiencies of our past, but we must also in the shortest possible time attempt to catch up with modern techniques.'

Of first importance was education. Without educated, well-trained people Ghana's development plans could not be carried out. Before the CPP government, there were not nearly enough schools or training colleges, and there was no university. But within ten years of CPP rule more had been done to extend education than in a hundred years of colonial rule.

In every part of Ghana new schools and training colleges were built, and the University of Ghana was opened at Legon. Soon there were also universities at Kumasi and Cape Coast. Every child in Ghana could go to school, and all had a chance to go on to a training college or to university. The parents did not have to pay any fees. All education from primary to university level was made free; and all textbooks were supplied by the government free of charge to children in primary, middle and secondary schools.

For a time there was a shortage of teachers because of the big increase in the number of schools, and of children attending school. Work was begun on the building of more teacher training colleges. In the meantime, Radio Ghana helped with its regular school broadcasts.

A specially powerful broadcasting station was set up to carry the voice of Ghana to every part of Africa and beyond. At first, broadcasts were in English and French, but soon the station was sending out news bulletins in the main African languages.

Between 1957 and 1966, so many things were done to improve the health and happiness of the people that Ghana was widely recognised as having one of the highest standards of living in Africa. But there was still a long way to go. For example, many people still suffered from bad housing, insufficient food, and from diseases like malaria which could be prevented. Whole areas of Ghana were regularly sprayed to kill mosquitoes. But it would take time to get rid of malaria completely. The same applied to other problems and difficulties. No country can suddenly become a modern, industrialised state, or solve its social problems immediately. The important thing is to lay correct foundations, and to make steady progress towards improvement for all the people. This was being done in Ghana.

Remembering the poor state of the country when colonial rule ended, Nkrumah remarked: 'Those who would judge us merely by the heights we have achieved, would do well to remember the depths from which we started.'

8 : Problems and difficulties

One day, as Nkrumah was walking across the garden from his office in Flagstaff House, the sharp crack of a rifle shot rang out. It was quickly followed by another, and another. For a moment Nkrumah did not realise what was happening. Then, as the security officer beside him fell to the ground, dead, he suddenly spotted the man who was firing at them. He was a short distance away, partly hidden by a tree. In a second, Nkrumah was after him. Terrified, the man dropped the gun and ran off as fast as he could. But Nkrumah was too quick for him. Catching up with him round the side of the house he grabbed him and pulled him backwards to the ground.

The noise of the shots had alerted other security guards. But as they came running up, Nkrumah was already kneeling astride the man, firmly holding him down. The guards were amazed to see that the man Nkrumah had captured was a policeman who had been on guard duty at Flagstaff House. He was well known to them as a skilled marksman. They could not, therefore, understand how he could have missed hitting Nkrumah when he fired at him at such a short distance. Nkrumah had been walking slowly, and he was such an easy target in his white drill suit.

This attempt to kill Nkrumah happened on 1 January 1964. Shortly afterwards, two bandsmen in the police band reported that certain people had tried to persuade them to shoot Nkrumah when he approached the band to congratulate them on their performance. He always went over to congratulate the bandsmen when they had played at Flagstaff House.

Before then, in 1955, and again in 1958, there were plots to kill him. In 1955 a bomb was placed against his house in Accra. It went off, but no one was injured. In 1958, the plan was to carry out a coup. This meant overthrowing the government by force. Nkrumah was to be shot at Accra airport as he was about to leave for a state visit to India. The day before the coup was to take place, the plan was discovered and the plotters arrested.

But the most serious attempt on Nkrumah's life occurred in August 1962. Nkrumah was at Kulungugu in northern Ghana. He was returning from a visit to Upper Volta, and had got out of his car to speak to a group of children among the crowd which had gathered in the village to greet him. Suddenly, there was a loud bang. Someone had thrown a bomb close to where Nkrumah was standing. People screamed as smoke and dust filled the air, and everyone tried to run away from the place. The bodies of several people, including a child, lay on the ground. Others were bleeding from cuts caused by splinters from the bomb.

When the smoke and dust cleared, Nkrumah could be seen still standing in the same place, shocked at what had happened, but apparently uninjured. The people of Kulungugu did not know that several pieces of the bomb had gone into his back, and that he was in considerable pain. There was no hospital near, so he went to a local clinic. A doctor operated on him, cutting out one by one the bomb splinters from his back. It hurt greatly because Nkrumah refused to have anything to deaden the pain. He wished to remain alert in case another attempt was made to kill him.

Most Ghanaians were very angry at the attempts to kill Nkrumah, and wanted strong measures to be taken against those who opposed the government. They knew that most of them were people who wanted to follow the customs and methods of the British, which they had been taught to respect and admire. These were people with a colonial mentality. Many were members of parties which had failed to win any of the general elections of 1951, 1954 and 1956. Some of them were former members of the UGCC or the NLM, parties which had opposed Nkrumah and the CPP right from the start. These discontented people seemed to have given up hope of ever winning an election, and so had resorted to lies and violence in order to bring down the government. They had joined together in a single party, the United Party.

Through their newspapers, they carried on a vicious press campaign against Nkrumah and leading members of the CPP. They complained that money was being wasted, and that people were no longer free to do as they pleased. They pointed to shortages of certain goods in the shops and said it was the government's fault. They tried to stir up trouble by reporting all kinds of rumours and scandals in an attempt to make Ghanaians believe that the CPP were ruining the country.

Leaders of the United Party came mostly from families which had enjoyed a good standard of living even in colonial times. They hoped that when colonial rule ended they would step into positions occupied by the British, and would enjoy even greater privileges. It was a shock to them to realise that Nkrumah and progressive members of the CPP aimed to make basic changes in Ghana to give everyone a fair chance. Nkrumah, they said, wanted to turn Ghana into a socialist country. They were correct. Nkrumah frequently spoke about socialism. The resources of Ghana, he said, belonged to the people. They would plan how they could be developed and used for the benefit of everyone. Each would do the work for which he was best suited. Those who could not work, the old and the sick, would be taken care of.

'We aim', Nkrumah declared, 'at creating in Ghana a socialist society in which each will give according to his ability, and receive according to his needs.'

In a socialist state, the ordinary people would govern and no one would occupy a privileged position. This the opposition feared more than anything.

But it was not until the activities of those who opposed the government began to put the development plans at risk that action was taken against them. By then some thirty innocent people had been killed in bomb-throwing incidents. As Nkrumah said: 'We could not allow a small minority of unprincipled men to stir up disunity and confusion with the object of overthrowing the government, which had the support of the overwhelming majority of the people of Ghana.'

It became necessary to stop newspapers from printing distorted and untruthful news items. In addition, a law was passed, the Preventive Detention Act, which enabled the police to arrest and detain people without trial if they were suspected of crimes against the government and people of Ghana. But no one was executed for political reasons during the whole period of Nkrumah's rule. Even those found guilty of the bomb attack at Kulungugu were not killed. When he heard that the judge had sentenced them to death, Nkrumah after two weeks of fasting and meditation, spared their lives.

The fact that the vast majority of Ghanaians supported the government had been shown in three general elections. It was shown again in 1960 when Ghana became a republic, and Nkrumah was voted the first president. The party wanted him to be president for life, but he refused. He said that the people must have the opportunity of voting for a new president every four years. In 1964, Ghanaians voted to make the CPP the only party in Ghana. This was done to enable the government to go ahead with its development plans without being slowed up by an opposition which represented a very small part of the population.

Ghana was one of the first countries in Africa to become a one party state. At the time, some people said that it was wrong to allow only one party. But since 1964, many other countries, particularly in Africa, South America and Asia, have become one-party states. They have found it a more suitable form of government for their particular conditions. Most of them are former colonies, and have therefore to develop their countries very rapidly if they are to catch up with other parts of the world. They cannot allow small, selfish groups to stand in the way of measures designed to improve living standards for all the people.

Nkrumah knew that it would not be an easy task to carry out the development plans.

'Socialism', he said, 'cannot be built without socialists.'

It was essential, therefore, to set to work immediately after independence to make sure that everyone would know and understand what needed to be done if the resources of Ghana were to be fully developed for the well-being of all the people. It was necessary to train party members to discuss the government's plans with people in towns and villages, offices, shops, factories, farms, schools and colleges throughout Ghana.

An Institute was built at Winneba where party members could learn and discuss the aims of the CPP and party organisation. Soon, students and freedom fighters from other countries went to Winneba to attend courses designed to help them in their struggle to free their people. Nkrumah himself often went to Winneba to talk with the students and to take part in discussion groups. There was no excuse for any party member who had studied at Winneba not to know the party's aims and policies.

But there were some leaders of the CPP who became proud, and more interested in making money and building big houses for themselves than in serving the people. These greedy men gave the party a bad name, and betrayed the trust the people had placed in them.

In a broadcast made at dawn on 8 April 1961, Nkrumah told Ghanaians that self-seekers and those who cheated the people would be found out and dealt with very severely. Any possessions which they had acquired dishonestly would be taken away from them. In future, there would be strict limits placed on how much property party officials could own. No minister or member of parliament could be a businessman. All must live simply and modestly, like the people who had elected them.

'Some of us very easily forget', he said, 'that we ourselves have risen from amongst the masses.'

After the dawn broadcast several CPP ministers had to resign. Others were made to change their ways, and to give up most of their property.

In some respects, it was easier to end colonial rule than to stop the activities of Ghanaians who wanted to maintain their positions of power and privilege. The white colonist could be clearly seen, and Ghanaians were united in their efforts to end colonialism. It was a different matter after independence when it came to dealing with Ghanaians who in many secret ways tried to undermine the government. Some were businessmen. Others might be civil servants, lawyers, teachers, dishonest members of the CPP, or officers in the army and police.

They were not large in numbers, but they were in positions where they could do a lot of harm. For example, a big businessman could cause shortages of certain goods in the shops, or charge very high prices, and people would blame the government. A top civil servant could delay, or fail to carry out, an important government measure which he disliked. A university teacher could stir up trouble among students. A dishonest member of the CPP could spread confusion and distrust.

The problem of dealing with these trouble makers was made more difficult because they had the support of neocolonialists. These foreign businessmen opposed the policies of the CPP government because they wanted to continue to make a lot of money for themselves. They could not do this if the people of Ghana owned and controlled everything. Also, neocolonialists did not like the way the CPP government was developing new and wider trade links with other countries. Before independence, most of Ghana's trade was with Britain and with countries of western Europe and America. Neocolonialists wanted this pattern of trade to continue. For if the CPP succeeded in its aim of achieving economic independence it would mean an end to neocolonialism in Ghana. Furthermore, Ghana's progress towards economic independence and socialism was being closely watched by other African nations. Western business interests stood to lose if those countries adopted socialist policies.

Neocolonialists, therefore, encouraged and helped those Ghanaians who like themselves did not want to see basic changes in Ghana after independence. Together, they were able in all kinds of ways to make things difficult for the CPP government.

Nkrumah wrote a book called *Neocolonialism*. In this book he showed how foreign companies and governments were enriching themselves at the expense of the African people; and interfering in the affairs of independent states. When the book was published in 1965, the American government was so angry at what Nkrumah had written that a strong letter of protest was sent to the Ghana government. In addition, the Americans stopped the sending of 35 million dollars' worth of goods which they had promised to supply.

It is specially easy to find things to criticise when a country is going through a period of rapid change. There are bound to be problems and difficulties. Everyone must be prepared to suffer a little and to make sacrifices while development plans are being carried out. Nkrumah said the Seven Year Development Plan was like a planted seed. A seed takes time to grow. First, the ground must be prepared. For a time after the seed is planted, nothing shows. But all the time the farmer works hard on the land so that when the young plant does appear it will be strong and healthy. Gradually, the seed grows, until as a result of all the patient work and careful planning it eventually develops into a fully grown and beautiful plant which everyone can see.

By the beginning of 1966, there was already plenty of growth to see in Ghana. New factories, state farms, roads, universities, schools, hospitals, Tema harbour and township were all evidence of Ghana's progress. The great Volta dam was finished. The people of Ghana were showing that they were determined to develop their country through their own efforts, and in their own way, in spite of the opposition of neocolonialists and the selfish few who thought only of themselves.

In the words of Nkrumah: 'We were on the threshold of a great new victory. We had in 1957 won our political independence after eight years of struggle. Now in 1966 we were at the threshold of winning our economic independence.'

9 : Coup d'état on 24 February 1966

'Mr President, I have bad news. There has been a coup d'état in Ghana.'

'What did you say?' asked Nkrumah.

'A coup d'état in Ghana,' repeated the Chinese ambassador.

Nkrumah was in Peking. The date was 24 February 1966.

He had left Accra on 21 February, and was on his way to Hanoi, the capital city of Vietnam at the invitation of Ho Chi Minh, who was then the president of Vietnam. At that time, the people of Vietnam were fighting for their freedom against the forces of the United States of America. Nkrumah carried proposals for ending the war. He was at the farthest point of his journey, and well beyond any hope of a quick return to Ghana.

The ambassador went on to tell Nkrumah details of the news reaching them from Accra. At 6 am, he said, an army officer named Kotoka had declared on Accra radio that the army and police had taken over the government of Ghana.

The coup began during the night of Wednesday, 23 February 1966 when about 600 soldiers stationed at Kumasi were ordered to move southwards to Accra. On the way they were met by two officers, Afrifa and Kotoka. Afrifa was left in command while Kotoka went ahead to Accra to report progress to Harlley, the commissioner of police.

The troops were told that Nkrumah intended sending them to the war in Vietnam, and also to fight against the white settlers in Rhodesia. Nkrumah, they said, had left Ghana with £8 million and would not return. It was the duty of the army, therefore, to take over the government of the country to maintain law and order, and to prevent economic chaos.

Kotoka with 25 soldiers hurried to the home of the army chief of staff, Major-General Barwah. Barwah refused either to join the rebels or to surrender. Kotoka thereupon shot him dead in front of his wife and children. Seven soldiers on guard duty at Barwah's house were also killed.

While Kotoka and his men were dealing with Barwah, other rebel soldiers and police were arresting important government officials and seizing control of the airport, cable office, radio station, and all approach roads to Accra. At the same time, soldiers of the Accra garrison were ordered to take Flagstaff House. This proved to be no easy task because it was guarded by trustworthy soldiers of the President's guard regiment. These soldiers, although heavily out-numbered, bravely fought the rebel soldiers. For a time it seemed as though they might win. But further troops were sent to help the rebels. The outer walls of Flagstaff House were blasted open. Still they fought on. But eventually, after many hours, the loyal defenders had to give in. Many were killed. Others were beaten and taken prisoner.

Rebel soldiers rushed from room to room smashing windows and furniture, and destroying government records. They made a bonfire of precious books and papers in Nkrumah's office, and stole clothes and little personal things in his house. Nkrumah's wife and three small children were not harmed, but they were forced to leave Flagstaff House without taking anything with them. A few days later they left Ghana and went to live in Cairo. His mother Nyaniba, who was then eighty years old and almost blind, was also compelled to leave Flagstaff House. She was rudely told to go back to the village of Nkroful. Later, the rebels tried to make her say that Nkrumah was not her son. She refused to tell such a lie, and bravely said that she was determined to stay alive to see her son return to Ghana.

In the days which followed the coup, all CPP ministers, party officials and loyal supporters of the CPP government throughout Ghana were arrested and thrown into prison. Many were ill-treated. Those who seized power in Ghana on 24 February 1966 described it as a 'bloodless coup'. It was certainly not bloodless, though it may never be known for certain exactly how many people were killed or injured.

In Peking, Nkrumah immediately cancelled his visit to Hanoi, and ordered officers and men of the Ghana army to return to their barracks. In a statement read to the press he said: 'I am the constitutional head of the Republic of Ghana, and the supreme commander of the armed forces. I am returning to Ghana soon.' He then sent a cable to all Ghanaian embassies:

'Be calm and remain at your posts. Send all messages and reports to me through the Ghana embassy, Peking, and not, repeat not, through Accra until further notice.'

But as he discussed the coup with party officials who were with him, Nkrumah was disappointed to discover that most of them were frightened. All they seemed able to think about were themselves, their families and their property. How different was the attitude of the 66 security men and office staff who had travelled with him. They were not prepared to accept the coup and the betrayal of the Ghanaian people. They, like Nkrumah, were determined to fight back.

The Chinese made arrangements for Nkrumah to leave Peking as soon as possible. Meantime, he carried out the engagements planned for him. Clearly, the Chinese government thought the coup in Ghana no more than a temporary setback.

'You are a young man,' the Chinese prime minister, Chou En-Lai told Nkrumah. 'You have another forty years ahead of you.'

Messages of support arrived for Nkrumah from all over the world. Among African heads of state who expressed their support at this time were Sékou Touré of Guinea, Gamel Abdul Nasser of Egypt, Julius Nyerere of Tanzania, Milton Obote of Uganda, Modibo Keita of Mali, and the prime minister of Sierra Leone, Albert Margai.

President Sékou Touré in his message said that it was important to strike back without delay. He invited Nkrumah to go at once to Guinea:

'We are impatiently waiting for you.'

Nkrumah decided to accept the invitation from Sékou Touré and the people of Guinea. Apart from the fact that Ghana and Guinea had formed a union in 1958, Nkrumah wanted to go to a country as close to Ghana as possible. In a note dated 25 February 1966, he wrote to Sékou Touré:

> My dear Brother and President,
>
> I have been deeply touched by your message of solidarity and support I have received today. It is true, as you say, that this incident in Ghana is a plot by the imperialists, neocolonialists and their agents in Africa. As these imperialist forces grow . . . using traitors to the African cause against the freedom and independence of our people, we must strengthen our resolution and fight for the dignity of our people to the last man and for the unity of Africa. It is heartening to know that in this struggle we can count on the support and under-standing of Africa's well-tried leaders like yourself.
>
> I know that our cause will triumph and that we can look forward to the day when Africa shall be really united and free from foreign interference . . .
>
> I am safe and well here in Peking, and I have sent my special emissary who will deliver this message to you to let you know the plans I am making for my early return to Africa.
>
> I shall visit you in Guinea soon.
>
> With sincere and brotherly affection,
>
> Kwame Nkrumah

The government of the Soviet Union sent an aircraft to Peking to fetch Nkrumah and his party, and on 28 February they left China. The first stop was Irkutsk in Siberia. Then on they flew to Moscow where they landed at dawn on the first of March. There they were welcomed by Soviet leaders. The whole day was spent discussing future plans, and it was not until midnight that the aircraft took off for the flight to Guinea. After brief stops in Yugoslavia and Algeria they reached Conakry. It was then the afternoon of Wednesday, 2 March 1966.

Sékou Touré and a large crowd had gathered at the airport to welcome Nkrumah. As he stepped from the plane a 21-gun salute was fired, the greeting reserved for heads of state. It was the Guinean people's way of letting Nkrumah know that they did not accept the coup, and still regarded him as President of Ghana.

The following day, a mass rally was held in the stadium in Conakry. Sékou Touré and Nkrumah were driven round the arena in an open car. The people cheered and waved banners with the words: 'Long live Nkrumah', 'Long live Sékou Touré', and 'Down with neo-colonialism'.

Nkrumah was happy to be in Guinea. He felt at home as long as he was on African soil. But he was quite unprepared for Sékou Touré's speech that day. For Sékou Touré told the crowd that the government and people of Guinea had decided to appoint Nkrumah head of state of Guinea:

'The Ghanaian traitors', he said, 'are mistaken in thinking that Nkrumah is simply a Ghanaian.'

He told them that Nkrumah belonged to all the people of Africa, and that he, Sékou Touré, would be proud to serve under him. Sékou Touré spoke in French, and at that time Nkrumah did not know the language well. He knew from the excitement and the cheering of the crowd that he had been presented to them, and that an important announcement had been made. But it was not until afterwards that he realised exactly what Sékou Touré had said.

Nkrumah was deeply moved. No head of state had ever before declared that he would step down to make way for another leader from a different country. It showed to the world what the people of Guinea thought of Nkrumah and all he had done for African liberation and unity. It was, as Nkrumah said, 'a great landmark in the practical expression of Pan-Africanism'.

Nkrumah thanked Sékou Touré and the people of Guinea for their welcome and support. But he felt able to accept only the position of joint President. He therefore became co-President of Guinea.

For the next six years, Nkrumah lived in a house on the sea-front, called Villa Syli, about a mile from the centre of Conakry. In the distance to the east he could see the hills of Sierra Leone; in the other direction, the shores of Guinea Bissau. At that time, Guinea Bissau was still a colony of Portugal, and a people's war was in progress to free the country. The freedom fighters were led by Amilcar Cabral.

Cabral and freedom fighters from other parts of Africa often visited Nkrumah in Conakry. They spent many hours discussing not only their particular problems but the whole question of African liberation and unity, and ways to end all forms of injustice. It was said that more freedom fighters passed through Villa Syli than visited Flagstaff House when Nkrumah was in Ghana.

Within a few weeks of his arrival in Guinea, Nkrumah had set up an office in Villa Syli, and a radio station so that he could keep in close touch with developments in Ghana and the rest of the world. For a time he broadcast regularly to the Ghanaian people:

'The rebellion by certain army and police officers in Ghana was directed not only against Ghana, but also against the African Revolution and the unity and independence of our continent,' he told them.

'Stand firm and organise.'

The 79 Ghanaians who had accompanied him to Guinea, and others who joined him later, were each given a job to do. Those with police or army training helped Guinean forces to protect Villa Syli. Those skilled as clerks or secretaries were employed in the work of

Co-Presidents of Guinea, Kwame Nkrumah and Sékou Touré celebrating May Day with the people of Guinea in the stadium in Conakry on 1 May 1967

Nkrumah's office. Others attended to the day to day work of the Villa. No one was idle. Ali had to undergo courses of military training, and to attend political discussion classes. Nkrumah wanted everyone to be fully prepared for the struggle which lay ahead. For he was determined to return to Ghana to carry on from there the fight for African liberation and unity.

He studied methods of guerrilla warfare, and trained with units of the Guinean forces. Soon he became quite a good marksman. He learned to drive, and had French lessons. But much of his time was taken up with writing books. When the coup took place in Ghana, seven had already been published. While he was in Conakry he wrote six more. First, he finished work on *Challenge of the Congo*, a book in which he showed how foreign interference in the Congo (now Zaire), led to the murder of Patrice Lumumba, and threatened the whole of independent Africa. Next, he wrote the *Handbook of Revolutionary Warfare*, a guide for African freedom fighters. In the same year, a freedom fighters' edition of *Axioms* was published. This was a little pocket book containing key passages from his speeches and writings.

There followed *Dark Days in Ghana*, a book about the Ghana coup of 1966. Nkrumah examined the reasons for the coup, its results in Ghana, and the way it had affected the freedom struggle in other parts of Africa. He described the progress made in Ghana since independence, and how the development plans were beginning to show results. Those who carried out the coup had told a 'big lie' when they claimed that Ghana needed to be rescued from economic chaos. Certainly, there were plenty of problems still to be solved. The price of cocoa had fallen to a very low level. There were shortages of certain goods in the shops. Everyone was being asked to tighten their belts, and to give up a measure of personal freedom to enable socialist planning to go ahead. These and similar problems face most countries which have to develop rapidly after a long period of colonial rule.

'I have written', Nkrumah said, 'about Ghana's "dark days" in the hope that publication of the facts may help expose similar setbacks in other progressive independent African states.'

Two years later, came *Class Struggle in Africa,* a short but very important book which he dedicated to 'the workers and peasants of Africa'. This book was written after there had been a succession of army coups in Africa. Twenty-five took place between January 1963 and December 1969. Nkrumah showed the close links between neo-colonialists and those Africans who opposed parties with socialist policies.

'As long as violence continues to be used against the African peoples', he wrote, 'the party cannot achieve its objectives without the use of all forms of political struggle, including armed struggle.'

While he was writing these books, Nkrumah was also making notes for a further two books, one on Zimbabwe, and the other to be called *Revolutionary Path.* He did not have time to finish them, and they were published after his death.

The books Nkrumah wrote, and the broadcasts he made, encouraged Ghanaians to resist the government of army and police officers which had been forced upon them after the coup. This government, calling itself the National Liberation Council (NLC), tried to stop people listening to the broadcasts, and many radio sets were seized by the police. But people listened in secret and passed on Nkrumah's messages.

Soon, several attempts were made to capture or kill Nkrumah. One night, when it was very dark, a Guinean naval patrol ship discovered a strange fishing boat close in-shore near to Villa Syli. They stopped it and arrested those on board. They were found to be criminals specially released from Ghanaian prisons and sent to kidnap Nkrumah. They were to take him back to Ghana, dead or alive.

But no matter how they tried, the NLC could not silence Nkrumah. His voice from Conakry continued to be heard:

'Workers, farmers and peasants in all parts of Ghana, organise and act now. You have to liberate your country once again as you did in the days of British colonialism. Your goal is historic – it is the building of a society in Ghana within a united socialist Africa. Workers, farmers and peasants of Ghana do not despair or fear the future. Act NOW. The struggle continues.'

10 : In Conakry

Nkrumah was sitting outside his office at Villa Syli. The sea was heaving gently up against the grey stone wall of the terrace. It was early evening and a light breeze was blowing. He looked at his watch:

'Buah,' he called, 'Buah, the radio please.'

Buah was already hurrying to bring the radio, switched on and tuned to Radio Ghana. For he knew that Nkrumah would want to listen, as he always did, to the daily news broadcast from Accra. He placed the radio on the small table beside Nkrumah, and waited to hear the drumming which always preceded the reading of the news.

'Thank you,' said Nkrumah.

The drumming began, and both knew the radio was tuned correctly. Buah was about to leave.

'Wait and hear the headlines,' Nkrumah said.

He turned the volume up a little as the sound of drums faded away and the voice of the Ghanaian news reader announced the start of the bulletin.

'In an agreement signed today', he began, 'Ghana's state rubber plantation was sold to the Firestone Company of America. The 20-square-mile plantation, in the western region' . . .

Nkrumah heard no more.

The U.S. Firestone Company? The very same company which owned the huge rubber plantations of Liberia? This company was now the owner of the precious rubber plantation which belonged to the people of Ghana?

Nkrumah covered his eyes with his hand.

The young rubber trees had been specially planted a few years ago to provide rubber for Ghana, and to sell to other countries. The money from exports of rubber would help to buy machinery and other goods needed for Ghana's growing industries. The trees were just beginning to produce rubber. Now, the results of all the planning and hard work of Ghanaians belonged to Americans?

'Ghana, Ghana,' Nkrumah murmured.

Without a word, Buah slipped away.

Each day there seemed to be fresh news of the abandonment of the Seven Year Development Plan. The NLC was allowing one state-owned industry after another to pass into private hands. Among those sold were the Timber Products Corporation, the Cocoa Products Corporation, the Diamond Mining Corporation, the national steel works and all the publicly owned hotels. Businessmen from the USA, Britain, West Germany and elsewhere travelled to Ghana as Nkrumah said, 'like vultures to grab the richest pickings'.

At the same time, work was stopped on the building of several new factories. For example, the half-completed Juapong textile and knitting factory near Akosombo was abandoned. This factory was planned to produce cloth using cotton grown on Ghanaian state farms. The Chinese experts who had been helping with the factory were sent home by the NLC. Six months later, it was almost impossible to see the unfinished buildings because weeds had grown all over them.

The NLC also expelled Soviet technicians who had been invited to Ghana to help with various development projects. At the time of the coup, some of them had been servicing Soviet-built fishing trawlers. These had been bought to enable Ghanaian fishermen to catch more fish to improve the diet of the people. At first, the NLC declared that the trawlers would be returned to the Soviet Union. Later, when many Ghanaians protested, they decided to sell the trawlers to local businessmen. Altogether, about 2,500 Soviet and Chinese experts who were helping with development work were expelled from Ghana by the NLC.

Neocolonialists and Ghanaians who had welcomed the overthrow of the CPP government were delighted. Ghana, they hoped, would now develop in the way they wanted. It would depend on aid from the West, and would move away from socialist and Pan-African policies.

The International Monetary Fund (IMF) and the governments of the USA, Canada and West Germany were among the first to make generous loans to Ghana. Furthermore, the price of cocoa in world markets suddenly rose again, after having dropped to a very low level just before the coup.

The very poor price paid for cocoa had been one of the main causes of economic difficulty leading up to the coup. The Seven Year Development Plan had been worked out on the basis of a price of at least £200 a ton. It was reasonable to expect this in view of price levels of previous years. But in 1965, the price suddenly fell to £87 a ton, compelling the CPP government to take unpopular economy measures to safeguard the development projects. With the support of their Western friends and the much better prices paid for Ghanaian cocoa, the NLC were able to strengthen their position.

When the coup occurred, most Ghanaians except those living in Accra were taken by surprise. The first thing they heard was Kotoka's broadcast at 6 am on Radio Ghana when he announced the overthrow of the CPP government. By the time people realised what had happened, it was all over. The CPP was banned. Party leaders had been arrested and the NLC were firmly in control of the country.

There was no people's militia to oppose the army and police units which carried out the coup. Plans had been made to form one, but there was not time to carry them out before Nkrumah left for Hanoi. The people were, therefore, unarmed and untrained to resist a violent overthrow of the government.

Another reason for the lack of CPP resistance was the low level of political knowledge, and the weakness of CPP organisation. In general, the people did not realise the full meaning of the coup. They thought in terms of a change perhaps bringing easier living conditions, and less discipline and hard work. Once their leaders had been arrested, and with Nkrumah out of the country, they were lost. The Institute at Winneba had been founded for the political education of the masses. But again, there had been insufficient time to achieve significant results.

During the months that followed the coup, attempts were made by the NLC to convince Ghanaians and world opinion that Nkrumah and the CPP government were inefficient and corrupt. In order to do this, they set up commissions of enquiry to examine in public various aspects of CPP rule. In a few cases the commissioners exposed genuine misgovernment and corruption on the part of certain members of the CPP. But in general, they failed to do more than feed the local press and radio with a steady stream of gossip and abuse designed to justify the overthrow by force of the legal government.

Unable, or unwilling to attack the policies of Nkrumah and his government, the NLC tried to destroy his name by accusing him of almost every possible crime. He was said to be a dictator, a spendthrift, a thief and even a murderer. A description of him was put up outside police stations under the heading:

WANTED FOR MURDER

A reward of £50,000 was promised for his capture alive or dead. Newspapers and radio stations of the West gladly spread the stories.

In Rhodesia, the settler government was specially happy at the news from Ghana. Nkrumah was a strong supporter of the freedom fighters of Zimbabwe. He had called for armed force to be used against the settlers after they declared their independence (UDI) in November 1965. At the time of the Ghana coup, Nkrumah was planning joint action by the African states to end the settler rebellion, and to help the people of Zimbabwe to win their freedom.

In Ghana, the NLC closed down the freedom fighter training camps, after allowing foreign newsmen to visit them and to take photographs. Hundreds of freedom fighters fled from Ghana as soon as the coup took place. But many were arrested and imprisoned. Later, some were sent back to their countries of origin where they faced a possible death sentence.

The NLC struck against all persons and organisations connected with the Pan-African movement. The Bureau of African Affairs, the African Affairs Centre in Accra, and the Institute at Winneba were closed down. So also, was the All-African Trade Union Federation (AATUF).

Meantime, once they had recovered from the initial shock of the coup, Ghanaians began to meet secretly to discuss what to do. As state farms were closed down, and building work stopped on development projects, thousands of men and women became unemployed. Soon, the NLC abolished the free health service and free education provided by the CPP government. Parents were faced with rising prices for food, and in addition had to try to find money to pay for school fees and medical care.

Discontent grew.

In London, members of the Overseas Branch of the CPP encouraged resistance. On the day of the coup, they issued a statement condemning the army and police traitors and calling on foreign governments not to recognise the NLC:

'The party overseas remains organised and at its post', they declared, 'and calls for the continued support of all loyal Ghanaians for the legally elected leader, Osagyefo Dr Kwame Nkrumah.'

The name 'Osagyefo', meaning 'victorious leader', had been given to Nkrumah by Ghanaians in recognition of his leadership in the independence struggle.

As the months passed, and Nkrumah continued to listen to news from Ghana, he heard of strikes, demonstrations, the stealing of ammunition from army camps, and many other incidents which indicated that Ghanaians were actively opposing the NLC. Scarcely a week passed without the arrival in Guinea of a Ghanaian to tell Nkrumah about what was going on in Ghana. Some of them spoke of plans for a coup to overthrow the NLC. Others just wanted to join the staff of Villa Syli.

Then suddenly, at 6 am on 17 April 1967, a strange voice was heard on Radio Ghana. It was Lieutenant Samuel Arthur announcing that the NLC had been overthrown.

Lieutenant Arthur with the support of Lieutenant Moses Yeboah and Second Lieutenant Osei Poku and some 120 men had entered Accra during the night. They had captured the radio station, Flagstaff House, and entered Christiansborg Castle. The leader of the 1966 coup, Kotoka, had been killed.

When Arthur's broadcast was heard in Conakry, the Ghanaian

duty officer ran to tell Nkrumah. Knocking loudly on his bedroom door:

'There's been a coup in Ghana,' he called.

Nkrumah was already up, and was in the middle of his daily exercises. In a flash he unlocked the door.

Happily, and in great excitement the duty officer told Nkrumah what had happened. As he spoke, other Ghanaians came running up. They felt sure that the coup was to restore the CPP government, and they wanted Nkrumah to make an immediate broadcast to the Ghanaian people.

If Nkrumah was excited at the news, he did not show it. Calmly he told the men to be patient. The news from Ghana, he said, seemed to be good. But it was too early to be sure. They must await developments.

During the morning they listened anxiously to the radio for further announcements. Ghana Radio was continuing to broadcast military music. This was abruptly broken off at about ten o'clock when the voice of Harlley, the NLC police chief, declared that the coup attempt had failed. The coup leaders, he said, had been arrested, and the NLC was in full control again.

It appeared the coup had not been well planned, and the NLC had little difficulty in stopping it.

Lieutenants Arthur and Yeboah were sentenced to death by firing squad, and Second Lieutenant Poku to 30 years' imprisonment. The two brave young officers were shot in public on 9 May in front of a huge crowd. It was the first time that anyone had been publicly executed in Ghana. Ghanaians and friends of Ghana all over the world were deeply shocked.

Nkrumah was at the time writing his book *Dark Days in Ghana*. He decided to dedicate it:

> *To Major General Barwah, Lieutenant S. Arthur and Lieutenant M. Yeboah and all Ghanaians killed and injured resisting the traitors of the 24th February 1966.*

A year later, in 1968, the NLC declared its intention to return Ghana to civilian rule. But all political activity was forbidden for

In Conakry 1968. Kwame Nkrumah walks to his office in Villa Syli

another year, and the CPP remained banned. In addition, thousands of Ghanaians were to be barred from holding public office for ten years because they were members of the CPP.

Nkrumah urged the people of Ghana not to be deceived by the NLC:

'Having seized power by force', he said, 'they are never likely to hand over to a civilian government through a freely conducted general election. In the face of such a government they would stand condemned.'

In April 1969, General Ankrah, Chairman of the NLC, was accused of corruption and compelled to resign. His place was taken by Afrifa, one of the leaders of the 1966 coup.

The following month, the NLC lifted the ban on political activity which had been in force since 24 February 1966. Three new political parties were allowed. They were the Progress Party (PP), led by Dr Kofi Busia; the People's Popular Party (PPP), led by Dr Lutterodt; and the All People's Party (APP), led by Dr E. V. C. de Graft Johnson. But the CPP was still banned.

When the general election was held, on 29 August 1969, thousands of Ghanaians did not vote. Some were banned from voting because of their CPP record. Others refused to vote since they did not wish to support any of the three parties.

The result was a clear victory for the Progress Party. At long last, with the CPP banned, Busia's party had been able to claim an election victory. Busia became prime minister, and on 30 September 1969, military government ended in Ghana.

Ghanaians were glad to have a civilian government again. The leaders of military coups always declare that they will hand over to civilians as soon as they consider the time is right. But they very rarely do so.

However, as the months went by, Ghanaians found that the change made very little difference to their daily lives. The Progress Party, like the NLC, believed that Ghana should move away from socialism and Pan-Africanism, and should maintain close links with the West.

Living conditions for most of the people did not improve. Prices continued to rise, thousands remained without work, and the number of strikes increased. During a riot following a strike at Sambrebori, three people were killed.

In an attempt to provide more jobs for Ghanaians the Busia government declared that all foreigners without residence permits would have to leave Ghana within two weeks. Many thousands, most of them Nigerians, were compelled to give up their homes and their work to return to Nigeria. This caused much hardship and suffering, and did little to ease the unemployment problem in Ghana.

In most African countries there are workers from other states. These migrant workers, as they are called, usually work for a few years and then return home. In times of difficulty, it is easy to blame them for troubles which are not of their making.

'In Africa there should be no "alien",' said Nkrumah, 'all are Africans.'

But Busia did not share the Pan-African views of Nkrumah.

In March 1971, the Busia government, together with the governments of Ivory Coast, the Central African Republic, and the Malagasy Republic, accepted the South African government policy of 'dialogue'. This meant they were prepared to discuss apartheid and the whole question of the liberation of southern Africa with the South African government. The majority of African states did not trust the South African government, and did not believe that any real progress could be made through a policy of dialogue. They held that the Africans of southern Africa would be liberated through their own efforts. If the South African government wished to discuss apartheid it should be prepared to do so with the African people living in South Africa.

The Busia government became more unpopular when a treaty of friendship was signed with Ivory Coast in May 1971. The President of Ivory Coast, Felix Houphouet-Boigny, had been among the first to agree to dialogue with South Africa. As a result of student protests he had closed the University of Abidjan.

From being in the forefront of the Pan-African movement during the period of CPP rule, Ghana was now among those African countries known to be against fundamental change.

In July 1971, a new Ghana People's Party was formed in Accra. The following month, the Busia government found it necessary to pass a law to ban the restoration of Nkrumah or the CPP.

In Conakry, Nkrumah watched and prepared.

11 : 'Nkrumah lives and will live forever'

It was just before two o'clock on the morning of 22 November 1970. The night was very dark, and a thick mist was rising off the sea. All was quiet in Conakry.

Suddenly, a noise like thunder broke the silence. There it was again, and again. Everyone was awake now. What they heard was not thunder but the roar of heavy gunfire from Portuguese warships a few miles out to sea. Within seconds, shells were exploding along the shore near to the airport, and around the harbour. Under cover of the bombardment, and hidden by the sea mist, mercenaries were jumping from small boats on to the beaches.

It was the start of the invasion from Guinea Bissau which Sékou Touré had warned might happen at any time. In a broadcast at the end of October 1970, he had told the people about groups of Guinean exiles which had gathered in Ivory Coast and Senegal to prepare to link up with an invasion force being trained by the Portuguese in Guinea Bissau. The Guinean exiles had left the country because they were opposed to the policies of the Guinean Democratic Party (PDG). They were now, Sékou Touré said, joining Portuguese colonialists who were determined to overthrow his government to prevent any more help being given to the PAIGC, the liberation movement led by Cabral. The PAIGC had already freed large areas of Guinea Bissau, and the Portuguese feared that unless they destroyed their bases and supply lines in Guinea, they would soon lose the whole of their colony.

The people of Guinea were armed and ready for the invaders. As soon as the alarm was raised, men and women of the people's militia grabbed their weapons and ran to join units protecting key points in the city. Soldiers of the regular army rushed from their barracks to reinforce comrades guarding the harbour, airport, radio station, and the approach roads to Conakry. Everyone knew where to go, and what to do. Along the coast at Villa Syli, Guinean soldiers and Ghanaians took up battle positions.

One of the first places the invaders attacked was Belle Vue, the government guest house where Nkrumah had stayed when he first arrived in Conakry. They evidently thought he still lived there. They also attacked Cabral's house. But he was out of the country.

Nkrumah had woken at the first burst of gunfire. Immediately, he was on the telephone to Sékou Touré to find out if he was safe. He thought there might have been a coup in Conakry.

Heavy fighting was taking place at the airport and in the streets between Villa Syli and Sékou Touré's residence. Sékou Touré advised Nkrumah to make no attempt to join him, but to go at once to the North Korean embassy, a building next to Villa Syli. Nkrumah went there, but only stayed a few hours.

Members of the militia and soldiers of the regular army prevented the invaders from reaching Sékou Touré's residence in the centre of Conakry. The invaders also failed to take the airport or the radio station. Sékou Touré broadcast to the people, calling on them to carry on the fight:

'Foreign ships are still in our territorial waters,' he said. 'Hundreds and hundreds of European mercenaries of many nationalities are taking part in the attack. Many of these mercenaries are in the hands of the revolutionary forces, but the battle continues.'

The sound of his voice, strong and calm, encouraged the people to even greater efforts. They knew that he was safe, and directing the battle.

'Guinea', he declared, 'will never come under the domination of neocolonialism . . . Guinea will defend itself to the last drop of blood.'

He warned of traitors within Guinea who would try to assist the invaders, and appealed for the support of all the people of Africa.

As fighting continued, some of the mercenary leaders were

captured. When questioned, they told their captors details of the invasion plans. The intention was, they said, to capture key points in Conakry to prepare the way for further troops who were to be brought in by air. They had been told that they would be helped by Guineans who were against the PDG; and that there would be risings in other parts of Guinea.

All day the fighting went on, in the streets of Conakry, along the beaches, and in the open country around the airport.

Just after 4 pm, Conakry radio reported that members of the people's militia from other parts of Guinea were pouring into the capital to help their comrades:

'You are no longer alone. Your comrades in arms of other party branches and towns have come to join you. . . . The struggle is now general. The defence of the nation must now be a matter of life and death for us. Comrades, on with the struggle. . . . The imperialist aggression will be crushed this very day. Today we will either win or die.'

As it began to get dark, further attacks were expected. But by then, the Guinean people were in full control of Conakry, and were busy dealing with isolated groups of mercenaries who were holding out at various points along the coast.

That night, there was another attack from the sea. It was not a further invasion but an attempt to rescue mercenaries who had landed the night before, and who were assembling in small groups at various points, hoping to be picked up and taken back to the Portuguese warships.

Fighting continued during the following day and night. Then finally, the Portuguese warships left Guinean waters. Gradually, the remaining mercenaries stranded in Guinea were forced to surrender.

It was a great victory for the Guinean people. The invaders had been defeated. But there could be no relaxation until a thorough investigation had been carried out to discover the local traitors who had been prepared to help them.

Nkrumah and Sékou Touré were convinced that there were people occupying important positions in Guinea who were secretly against the socialist policies of the Guinean government. Many of them pretended to be keen supporters of the PDG while all the time they were undermining it. These people were similar to those in Ghana who supported the coup against the CPP government, and cooperated with neocolonialists. They were from families which had occupied comfortable positions during colonial times, and which did not wish to see progress towards socialism after independence.

As soon as the fighting ended, Nkrumah went to see Sékou Touré. It was one of their happiest meetings. But both knew that the people's victory was not complete. For the invasion attempt had shown the extent and depth of secret opposition to the PDG from within Guinea. The high degree of PDG organisation and discipline which had resulted in victory over the invaders, must now be turned towards solving this problem.

Some of the traitors had been captured during the fighting. Others were arrested later as the investigations proceeded.

People were shocked to discover that many of the prisoners had occupied important positions in the PDG and in the armed forces and police. Among the 300 or so people charged initially and found guilty, were 17 government ministers, 8 governors, 55 top civil servants and party officials, 20 members of the armed forces, and 7 foreigners.

They were tried by members of the National Assembly sitting as a People's Supreme Court. Nkrumah attended the Court, and with Sékou Touré at his side listened to the confessions of the prisoners and heard how they had plotted with Guinean exiles and with the Portuguese to overthrow the government.

As a result of the trial it was decided that branches of the PDG in every town and village should conduct their own enquiries to find out if anyone in their areas had been involved in the attack. During the weeks that followed, they sent their reports to the Central Committee of the party, and further trials were held. At the same time, measures were taken to tighten up party discipline, and to improve the political education of the people.

Nkrumah at this time was not well. For several months he had suffered from stomach upsets, and from severe pains in his back. Now he also had intermittent bouts of fever and was becoming very thin.

The doctors who examined him gave him medicines and injections. But he did not improve.

By the beginning of January 1971, he was so ill that Sékou Touré and the Ghanaians at Villa Syli tried to persuade him to go for treatment overseas. But he did not want to leave Guinea. He had reason to believe that a coup might take place before long in Ghana and that he would return to Accra. If he left Guinea for medical treatment, news of his illness was sure to be reported, and it might discourage the Ghanaian people. Furthermore, he hoped to be able to consult his own doctors once he was back in Ghana.

As the months went by the pain increased. Soon, he could hardly walk. Still he would not leave Guinea. When in August 1971, he finally agreed to go to Rumania for treatment he was so weak that he had to be carried to the aircraft.

Travelling with Nkrumah were two Ghanaians and a Guinean government officer named Camara Sana, who had been in attendance at Villa Syli ever since Nkrumah's arrival in Guinea.

Nkrumah was taken to a clinic on the outskirts of Bucarest. He was given a large room which overlooked a beautiful garden. Nkrumah had always liked to see flowers. But to the dismay of the doctors he did not move from his chair, facing the door and with his back to the windows.

The doctors told Nkrumah that they would have him walking again in two weeks' time. But the weeks went by and it seemed they could not cure him. He grew thinner, and the pain increased.

In October, he was moved to a hospital in the centre of Bucarest, where he had a small operation to help relieve the pain. The two Ghanaians went with him, and occupied an adjoining room. Nkrumah was now in bed all the time. But he never lost heart. He was determined to get well again so that he would be ready to return to Ghana to carry on his work.

Every day, as in Guinea, he would listen to the news and discuss it with the Ghanaians who were with him. On 13 January 1972, he heard news of the fall of Busia's government and the setting up of the National Redemption Council (NRC) as the result of a coup led by Colonel Acheampong.

'Aren't you happy to know that Busia has gone?' asked one of the Ghanaians.

'Half of me is happy,' Nkrumah replied. He paused. 'And now this,' he said, referring to his illness.

The Ghanaians said they thought the coup must be for him. But Nkrumah was not so sure.

'Have they sent for me?' he asked.

Sadly they had to admit that this had not been done.

It was Nkrumah's dearest wish to return home. When he became seriously ill in 1971, Sékou Touré sent two urgent messages to Busia's government informing them of the situation. Nothing was done. After the coup of 13 January 1972, the NRC were told that Nkrumah had only a very short time to live, and that he wished to return to Ghana. He did not ask for reinstatement, but simply to be allowed to see Nyaniba again, and to be among his own people. But again, no message or invitation was received.

Nkrumah died in Bucarest early in the morning of 27 April 1972. With great courage he had fought to recover. But the illness, which was said to be cancer, finally overcame him.

Two days later, his body was flown to Conakry. In a speech to the nation, Sékou Touré said: 'Nkrumah lives and will live for ever because Africa, which is grateful to him, will live for ever.'

The NRC asked the Guinean government to allow the body of Nkrumah to be sent to Ghana. Sékou Touré replied that agreement could only be given on certain conditions. The NRC must receive the coffin with all the honours due to a head of state. In addition, the NRC must proclaim openly that they intended to carry on the work of Nkrumah for the freedom and unity of the African people. Political prisoners must be released, and the Ghanaians in Conakry be allowed to return home.

For two days, on 13 and 14 May 1972, the people of Guinea and guests from all over Africa and other parts of the world attended funeral ceremonies in Conakry. Among them were many representatives of liberation movements. For the freedom fighters of Africa regarded Nkrumah as their greatest supporter. As soon as Ghana became independent in 1957, he had declared that Ghana would be a base area from which the total liberation and unification of Africa could be launched. Under his protection, freedom fighters organised and trained in Ghana. Nkrumah had given them help in their most difficult years when the struggle was hardest.

Addressing the mass meeting held in the People's Palace in Conakry on 13 May, Amilcar Cabral spoke of the 'cancer of betrayal' which he said had been responsible for Nkrumah's death.

'We, the liberation movements', he said, 'will not forgive those who betrayed Nkrumah. The people of Ghana will not forgive. Progressive mankind will not forgive.'

He went on: 'For us, the best homage we Africans can render to the immortal memory of Kwame Nkrumah is to strengthen vigilance at all levels of the struggle, to intensify it, and to liberate the whole of Africa. To succeed in the development of the economic, social and cultural progress of our peoples, and in the building of African unity; this was the fundamental objective of the actions and thought of Kwame Nkrumah.'

At a big rally in Conakry stadium, units of the Guinean armed forces, people's militia, youth and workers' organisations marched past the white gun carriage, covered in flowers, which bore the coffin of Nkrumah. Also marching in the procession were the Ghanaians from Villa Syli.

When the stadium ceremony ended, thousands of people followed the gun carriage to a park in central Conakry. There, the coffin was placed beside the tombs of Guinea's national heroes.

After nearly two months, the Guinean government finally agreed to allow the return of Nkrumah's body to Ghana, though the NRC had not fulfilled all the condition laid down by Sékou Touré. It was said that the intervention of the Nigerian government, and pressure from Nkrumah's family influenced the decision.

On 7 July 1972, the coffin was flown to Accra. Still standing at the airport was the statue of Kotoka, leader of the 1966 coup.

In Accra, a memorial service was held. The coffin was then taken for burial to Nkroful, Nkrumah's birthplace in western Ghana.

Nkrumah's mother, Nyaniba, tears running down her face, knelt beside the coffin. Members of the family placed her hands upon it. For she was totally blind, and had refused to believe that her son was dead. Although over ninety years old at the time of the coup, she had said that she would go on living until her son returned to Ghana. Now, her only wish was to die.

Kwame Nkrumah left a final message for the people of Africa. It formed the conclusion to his last book, *Revolutionary Path*, and was written in Bucarest a few months before he died. He began:

'The immense resources of Africa can only be fully utilised to raise the standard of living of the masses if our continent is totally liberated from all forms of oppression and exploitation, and if our economy is developed on a continental basis. . . . Colonialist and neocolonialist governments, racist settler regimes, and privileged groups in our society can be tolerated no longer.'

It had become necessary, to fight for total liberation and unification, he wrote, but the struggle still suffered from disunity. It was more urgent than ever before to bring Africa's armed forces and freedom fighters under a unified All-African party and military command.

He ended:

'The African people, in solidarity with comrades in every part of the world, have the means, the ability and the determination to banish once and for all, imperialism, neocolonialism, settler minority rule, and all forms of oppression from our continent. A unified and socialist society in which the African Personality will find full expression can and must be constructed. There is victory for us.'

Date summary

1909	18 September	Birth of Kwame Nkrumah
1927		Entered Teacher Training College in Accra
1930		Teacher in Elmina
1935		Arrived in America to attend Lincoln University
1945		Wrote *Towards Colonial Freedom*
„	May	Arrived in England
„	October	Fifth Pan-African Conference, held in Manchester
1947	14 November	Left England to return to the Gold Coast
1948	3 September	First edition of the *Accra Evening News* printed
1949	12 June	CPP launched in Accra
1950	8 January	Start of 'Positive Action'
„	22 „	Imprisonment in James Fort
1951	February	General election. CPP victory, Nkrumah elected for Accra Central
1951	12 February	Released from prison to form a government
1952	5 March	Became prime minister
1953	10 July	Motion of Destiny
1954	15 June	General election. CPP victory
1956	17 July	General election. CPP victory
1957	6 March	Independence of Ghana
1958	April	First Conference of Independent African States, held in Accra
1958	December	First All-African People's Conference, held in Accra. Ghana–Guinea Union

1960	December	Ghana became a republic
		Nkrumah first President
1961	8 April	Dawn broadcast
,,		Ghana–Guinea–Mali Union
1962		CPP 'Programme of Work and Happiness'
,,	August	Kulungugu bomb attempt on Nkrumah's life
1963		Publication of *Africa must Unite*
,,	25 May	Charter of the Organisation of African Unity signed in Addis Ababa
1964	11 March	Launching of the Seven Year Development Plan
1965		Publication of *Neocolonialism: the last stage of imperialism*
1966	23 January	First electricity began to flow from Volta River Project
,,	21 February	Nkrumah left Ghana for Hanoi
,,	24 February	Coup d'état. Overthrow of CPP government
		Setting up of National Liberation Council (NLC)
,,	2 March	Arrival of Nkrumah in Conakry
1967	17 April	Lt Arthur's attempted counter-coup in Ghana
1969	29 August	General election in Ghana. Busia's Progress Party in power
1970	22 November	Invasion of Guinea
1971	August	Nkrumah left Guinea for medical treatment in Romania
1972	13 January	Acheampong's coup. Fall of Busia's government
		Setting up of National Redemption Council (NRC)
1972	27 April	Death of Nkrumah in Bucarest
,,	13–14 May	Funeral ceremonies in Conakry
,,	7 July	Return of Nkrumah's body to Ghana